Paintball

Paintball

THE COMBAT ADVENTURE SPORT

RICHARD COOKE

WARD LOCK

To my wife Carol and my sons Adam, Andrew and Daniel

WARD LOCK
A Cassell Imprint
Villiers House, 41-47 Strand, London
WC2N 5JE.

Distributed in the USA by Sterling
Publishing Co. Inc., 387 Park Avenue
South, New York, NY 10016-8810.

Distributed in Australia by Capricorn
Link (Australia) Pty. Ltd, P.O. Box 665,
Lane Cove, New South Wales 2066.

British Library Cataloguing in
Publication Data
Cooke, Richard
Paintball: the combat adventure sport.
1. Adventure games
I. Title
796
ISBN 0-7063-7073-2

Designed and edited by DAG
Publications Ltd. Designed by David
Gibbons; edited by Michael Boxall;
layout by Anthony A. Evans; typeset by
Typesetters (Birmingham) Ltd, Warley,
West Midlands; camerawork by M&R
Reproductions, North Fambridge,
Essex; printed and bound in Great
Britain by The Bath Press, Avon.

ACKNOWLEDGEMENTS

Robert C. Waddington, Chief Executive: Western Tactical Systems; Jessica J. Sparks, Legal Counsel: International Paintball Players Association; Mary-Louise Littlefield, President: The Command Post. USA; R. H. Carden-Lovell, Managing Director: Major Paintball Industries; Harry Niece, Development Director: R. P. Scherer Ltd, England; Bill Aultman, Director: The Command Post UK Ltd; Paul Wilson, Chairman: Mayhem Paintball Games Ltd; David Byrne, Director: Ultimate Games (UK); Anthony Nelson MP: House of Commons, London; Richard Hockley, Hockbo Arms, Fort Collins, USA; B. Frier, Hi-Tech Industries, Kent; Officer Lovegrove, Firearms Dept. New Scotland Yard; I. Horton, Director: Encounters, Landford; Graham Barton: Battle Orders Ltd, Eastbourne; G. M. Kesler, President: National Gun Sports Corp, USA; E. Moffatt: Spell-Check-Services, UK; A. M. Mason: Scottish Home & Health Dept, Edinburgh; S. Baxter: Home Office, London; European Paintball Sports Federation UK Section; Fireball (Europe) Ltd, Antwerp, Belgium; A. & A. Cooke, Camera Crew (UK); A. Green, Commercial Sales Engineer: Brocks Explosives Ltd, Scotland; Pyro Supplies Ltd, UK.

Contents

Introduction

Most of us yearn for adventure but haven't the drive to accomplish it. Some, past and present, have chosen a professional military life as a means of finding danger and drama; others, because of wealth or privilege, have been able to undertake exploratory travel or adventurous exotic sports.

For many, however, the appetite for adventure is quickly dulled when danger is encountered. Our modern, anaesthetized lifestyle encourages pleasant day-dreaming from which harsh reality can provide a rude awakening. Perhaps what most of us might choose is adventure that is not painful, illegal or costly, and which is available close to home.

If such a formula could be found and could include the entire family, surely it would meet all requirements. Enter Paintball! – the adventure sport for everyone, where safety and enjoyment is paramount and even physical fitness is not a prerequisite. Even the competitive edge is adaptable, depending on the participants, and masculine strength is as likely to be a liability as an asset.

Since its birth in the USA in the 1980s, Paintball has largely been misunderstood by many people; the news media frequently branding Paintballers as 'survivalists, militarists and other radical groups of all kinds'. In fact, Paintballers are no different from any other sports people, except they may wear camouflage clothing to have fun in their sport.

▼ *Opposing teams stand and listen to the pre-game brief.*

Most of us can remember the adventure games of our childhood, playing cowboys and Indians, or even Star Trek, where one battled to save the Earth. The best thing about these childhood games was that no one ever got killed and when you had had enough everyone went home.

Paintball combines the fun of those childhood games, plus the excitement of an adult team sport, hi-tech weaponry and equipment, and tangible results. What other game allows you to stalk a human quarry that can, and does, shoot back? And one where if you achieve a 'hit' no damage is caused, and there is no dispute?

Paintball does not glamorize war or encourage people to be violent. In fact, in many ways it shows the players how easy it is to be shot and killed in a real combat situation when the bullets are live. Thus, the Paintball game is a deterrent to real warfare and highlights its futility.

As with all sports, Paintball will obviously not be to everyone's taste, but its players already come from all walks of life, are of all ages and include a high percentage of women. Many first-time players find the game more exciting than they would have thought possible.

How does Paintball compare with other sports?

Paintball rules prohibit any aggressive physical contact on the site or field. The game can be likened to a living video game or a living chess match, and relies on strategy and imagination rather than speed and strength. Women compete equally with men; neither

▶ **The enemy are spotted.**

7

age nor physical size is a barrier to becoming a good Paintball player. The game requires a small amount of physical ability, but people in wheelchairs, on crutches, or with missing limbs can compete successfully in Paintball. The Author is an asthmatic but manages to wheeze through even the toughest day's play.

Paint guns are available in both pump style and semi-automatic (one-hand operation) models and can be hired at most sites. Games run 15–45 minutes, depending on the size of the field and the number of players. On some sites a 'Big' game can last hours, but this is a specialist event.

Paintball is an easy sport to learn. After the safety rules have been explained, a beginner is generally playing the basic game ('Capture the Flag') within a matter of minutes; and novices will be especially overseen by the referees who supervise every game.

There are innumerable permutations to a game; no two contests are the same. Those who continue to play the game for years still feel the same challenge every time they walk out to a flag station and wait for the starting whistle.

Most regular players develop a real concern for the environment and an appreciation of the countryside because most Paintball games are played in fields, forests or wild areas (some scenarios are played indoors or in an urban setting, but on the whole, most games take place in the open). This must be of benefit to the player who spends the week working in an office or factory.

This book has been written with the aim of giving the novice some idea of just how much fun can be gained from Paintball, but the best advice is to try it! Feel the adrenalin pumping at the start of the game and the mixture of tiredness and achievement at its end. Who knows? You may have the Author in your sights one day!

▲ *The Author with the flag. Paintball in the snow.*

The Sport of Paintball

Early in 1988 I was commissioned by the magazine *Survival Weaponry and Techniques*, to look into the area of 'War Games', the unfortunate title by which 'Paintball' was known at the time.

The sport had few followers then, and the general public were completely ignorant of its growth until the tabloid press began using headline captions like 'Camo-Clothed Paramilitary Nutters Run Wild'. This type of coverage certainly captured public imagination, local councils held their breath, and police forces were warned to look out for this new weird craze that had come from America.

Within a few months, sanity was established, the Home Office set down guide-lines, the police could see the safety rules working, the press dropped the sensational headlines and the sport gently took root. At the start of 1990 there were 349 sites operating throughout the UK, all having many regular players. Taking an average game of twenty players, and by multiplying $20 \times 349 \times 52$ one arrives at the figure of 362,960 playing per year. Add to this the fact that a number of sites field large teams, with games being held on weekdays, the number of Paintball regulars in the UK could top the million mark.

Given this vast number of players, the sport has taken on a new look and the title 'War Games' has been lost together with the initial 'tacky' image. The sport status now achieved by Paintball has brought it permanence and respectability; it is now one of the most popular of the adventure leisure pursuits.

How do I get to play Paintball?

Most sites advertise in the specialist publications, local press and local radio often carry details, and even the national press has carried features and advertisements.

The normal way to get involved is to form a team of workmates or friends. Ideally, each team should have twenty players; the minimum is ten. The only requirement is that all the players be over the age of eighteen, but many sites now carry new insurance to accept younger players. Mixed, or women-only teams, are acceptable; Paintball is for both sexes and women play just as freely as men, often making deadly opponents. Should you find yourself on your own, or can only get two or three people together, most sites will fit you in in some way, usually by arranging for you to make up the numbers on an established team. Some sites have days when both teams are made up of individuals wishing to play.

What happens in a game of Paintball?

Paintball is an all the year round sport, played in any weather — rain, sleet, snow, hail or gale. Having played the game in some of the worst conditions Mother Nature can dish up, I must admit the rough weather made the game even more exciting; an opinion held by the majority of players. Most sites are located in wooded areas, though swamps, rocky outlets and sand dunes are sometimes used. At some locations derelict buildings are available for simulated urban environments. Prospective players should not be influenced by the size of a location, although the layout and terrain will govern the style of contest staged. The experience and professionalism of the site's staff will ensure that the best game is laid on.

The basic theme of Paintball is similar on all sites. The game is built around the idea of two teams trying to gain possession of their opponent's flag which is normally situated at the heart of each team's base camp. The winning team is the one that has the best organization, shooting skill and strategy, and achieves its objective in the fastest time. Defence and attack must be co-ordinated, so the game is one that tests mental skills as much as physical prowess. This is what makes the sport so attractive to such a vast cross-section of the public.

Good team work produces winning teams, so it is an advantage if you know the people alongside whom you are playing. Teams that practise together regularly often show best results at the close of a day's play. Owning a state of the art Paintball weapon is not the sole passport to success.

Origins

The concept of 'war games' or Paintball Sports originated in the United States in June 1981, utilising a piece of equipment originally intended for marking timber and livestock. Unlike the fill of today's paintball gun, the paint shot in the weapons at that time was an oil-based paint. If you got splatted with one of those balls it was a major job to remove the mark; you required a bottle of turps or the like to get it off exposed skin, and clothing carried the paint stains for ever. The stains did fade with time, but this ammo was made to last and lived up to its requirements.

The very first game was played on a 100-acre area, and was an every-man-for-himself game, each player starting at a different location and having to collect a flag from four different flag bases. The winner was the player who collected all four flags without getting shot. But the most amazing fact about this, the very first game, was that it was won by pure style and stealth by a New Hampshire forester, named Ritchie White, who was never once seen by the other eleven players, and who didn't fire a single shot.

A huge amount of publicity after this initial game caused the three players who thought of the idea, Charles Gaines, Hayes Noel and Robert Gurnsey, to form the group 'The National Survival Game Inc.' Paintball Games was born and the rest is history. Of course, the sport has moved on since those early days; the weaponry and equipment is changing weekly as technology changes, and fashion trends come and go.

Changes

One of the first innovations, after the game caught on, was to fill the gelatin balls with water-soluble colouring. This is still being done by the company that started it all, the Nelson Paint Company, of Iron Mountain, Michigan, USA. Today, half the company's business is concerned with supplying Paintball equipment. Charles Nelson, the company's co-founder, admits he has never played the game or ever seen it played. In the mid sixties he had invented a gun which could fire a paint pellet, as a tool for the lumber industry.

Straddling Michigan's north-west border with Wisconsin, Nelson's company has served the lumber industry since he and his brother started it in 1940, supplying paint for marking trees. 'Some foresters brought up the problem of marking trees from a distance, like across a river, and we began working on it,' he said.

Together with the Crosman Air Guns Company, they modified for Paintball use a pistol model that was designed to fire a dart to anaesthetize cattle. The problem was finding the right material for the Paintballs. 'A long process,' Nelson says. 'They were too hard or too brittle.'

When they finally got it right, they found the market wasn't there. 'The gun,' said Nelson, 'was much more expensive than other patented methods and perhaps the need wasn't as great as we were led to believe, although they're still being used by some foresters.' Meanwhile, the Crosman Company dropped out of the project causing Nelson to sign up with the 'Daisy Manufacturing Company', which still makes Nel-Spot Guns.

The business revived somewhat when cattlemen started buying the guns to mark animals for artificial insemination and other purposes. 'They had been using fishing poles with pieces of chalk fastened to the end,' said Nelson. Sales really took off, however, after the Paintball enthusiasts got involved. 'We thought it would be a fad thing that would die out after a year or so, but it's just growing all the time,' he said. The sport grew rapidly to the point where national leagues were established and hundreds of thousands of people now play the game on a regular basis with the supporting industry recording a turnover in excess of $800 million, and it's still in its growth phase.

The sport in Britain

Introduced into Britain in 1984, the sport had a slow start due to poor marketing and lack of public awareness, but within the last two years Paintball has enjoyed the expansion seen in other new leisure pursuits. The number of regular players has leapt to such a degree that there is already an acute shortage of sites – both existing and potential – to accommodate players.

As most people are aware, there is increasing pressure from National and European Government to find alternative uses for agricultural holdings, particularly in the area of leisure activities, and this sport provides the ideal opportunity to maximize income from acreage that previously returned very little, while not damaging the land itself.

▼ *Players suitably armed, camouflaged and protected.*

The following passage is an extract from my very first report from Mayhem War Games. The content of this report still holds good and true for any first-time player.

'MAYHEM WAR GAMES
Now in the '90s Mayhem is one of the largest Paintball Companies in the UK.

Mayhem changed their logo to 'Mayhem Paintball Games', and now run professional paintball sites throughout the country.

Land owners and local authorities with unusable rough scrub land can now reap the benefits of 'The Paintball Game' boom. Staging a Paintball Game on disused or unprofitable land can prove to be an attractive proposition to land-owners.

GAME SITE REQUIREMENTS
The specifications for a war-game site are relatively loose, but the minimum requirements are:

(1) The use of an area of woodland or broken ground of not less than eight acres, preferably with features such as gullies and streams.
(2) Access to the area by foot and vehicle (tractor, Land-Rover, etc.).

(3) A barn or outbuilding to act as reception and equipment-issuing centre.

(4) The playing site to be where the public have no right of access.

Having my three sons with me on this occasion, was a definite help as they bombarded Stephen (S. Baldwin, Director, Mayhem) with a barrage of questions which he answered and explained in full detail. Even the most basic questions from my youngest son, Daniel, were explained with ease.

Listening, I decided to take a few notes on the basic questions, the complete novice might ask:

Q. Can anybody play?

A. Yes, as long as he or she is aged 18 or over, has a sense of adventure, is basically fit, and wishes to spend a day participating in what will be the most stimulating game they are ever likely to have played.

Q. What do you bring?

A. Just a pair of comfortable strong boots or shoes, spare socks, a change of shoes for the drive home (a spare pair of jeans or trousers) and, don't forget, enthusiasm and a will to win.

Q. What are the rules?

A. As few as possible. There are, however, regulations to ensure your safety and a set of simple rules designed to enhance your enjoyment of the game.

Q. What are you given?

A. The use of a woodland site, the latest rapid-fire weapons, protective team clothing, armoured goggles, ammunition belt and holster, a supply of ammunition and CO_2, a hot lunch (for those playing all day) and the services of expert instructors and completely impartial umpires.

Q. Do I need to be experienced?

A. You will probably find that in the first game – as in any sport – it will take you time to come to grips with the tactics. However, the instructors are there to advise and point you in the right direction.

Q. Can I play as an individual?

A. Yes, on certain days we hold 'Open Season', where the teams are made up from individuals who wish to participate in this sport. Many players find these days particularly rewarding as it gives them the chance to meet new people and make new friends.

Q. What about the weather?

A. The conditions do not matter in the slightest. Many say the worse the weather the better the fun. You might get wet but you won't notice . . . the fun, excitement and adrenalin more than compensate for inclement conditions.

Q. Is it safe? (This is probably the most asked question world-wide).

A. Yes, as safe as any reasonably active participant sport can be. Provided that you observe the basic safety regulations, the worst you'll end up with will be a few scratches and aching muscles.

By this time the boys had run out of questions and it was time to round up for this first report. As I packed away my photographic gear, it was my wife Carol who asked Stephen if many women played the game. He replied that to date a good number of players had been women, and by all accounts once settled in they make 'pretty' formidable players.

End of report.

Mayhem Paintball Games Limited,
Head Office, Sunset Farm, Heathfield,
East Sussex TN21 OTX.'

Paintball Weaponry

The weaponry in this section is but a small selection of the many Paintball weapons currently available. It would be impracticable to mention every weapon on the market because the range available changes almost weekly. This selection is intended as a guide to those potential buyers who do not wish to spend an eternity in choosing a suitable weapon. When it comes to making your final choice, it is in your best interests to visit either a supplier or an on site Paintball shop, as this permits the crucial 'hands on' test to be made and greatly assists in the final decision. You may find that the 'ideal' gun as described in a magazine article does not suit you as far as handling and firing characteristics are concerned.

With this in mind the weapons in this section are in no order of preference, the tried and tested favourites being as impartially detailed as the latest additions to the ever-growing arsenal of weapons available. The Paintball gun market has grown so much that many serious players now buy their own guns with the result that a second-hand market of used weaponry is developing.

For the first-time buyer with no experience in what to look for, it is best to buy from a supplier or site owner as they have a reputation to uphold. In a private sale the novice may well buy poor quality and even dangerous equipment through ignorance of the leaky seals, worn actions and badly finished custom work. It is also prudent to get a weapon that you are considering purchasing chronographed, as this both ensures that it performs well and that it complies with the UK legal muzzle velocity limits. Law enforcement varies from country to country and the only sure authority is that of your local police force. A later section in the book goes into more detail on the Paintball law in various countries.

While every effort has been made to ensure the accuracy of information given in this book, the publishers and Author accept no liability for any innocent statement or error of fact concerning the laws governing Paintball weaponry.

THE NEL-SPOT PAINT GUN

The original Nel-Spot Paintball gun was developed from a liaison between the Nelson Paint Company, of Iron Mountain, Michigan, USA and the Daisy Manufacturing Company. The result was the 'Nel-Spot', still going strong and manufactured by the same company, now a world leader in air gun weaponry.

The year 1886 saw the first 'toy' air gun, the 'Chicago', launched by Markham Manufacturing Company, Michigan (a company later acquired by Daisy). The gun fired 'BB' shot, just 0.004 inches larger than present air rifle shot, and on 9 July 1888 it was decided to manufacture air rifles in limited numbers. Initially they were offered free to farmers who bought the company's iron windmill, but in 1889 the Daisy board decided to concentrate on air guns as its principal business. Daisy now has more than a century of air weapon design and manufacturing experience which is reflected in one of the world's best loved paint weapons.

NEL-SPOT 007 CHALLENGER

The Challenger reflects the latest state-of-the-art technology in Paintball guns. Its weight of 2.4 pounds is roughly half that of the original Nel-Spot 007, and it is constructed in highly resistant Nylafil with other durable materials. The solid brass barrel insert provides strength and durability yet is not affected by corrosion, rust and abrasion.

The Challenger uses gravity loading in that the paintballs are fed into the gun from a vertical tube magazine for immediate, trouble-free discharge. The new non-binding pump-action barrel, guiding handle and precision engineered parts make for smooth, rapid loading and cocking. The new 007 is far in advance of the old Mk 1.

The Challenger has a quick-change CO_2 cartridge fitted as standard and the new speed knob easily releases spent cartridges and rapidly locks in the replacement. For fast and easy field stripping, the thumbscrews, threaded barrel and slide-in breech assembly eliminate the need for tools. The Challenger possesses the point sight adapter as an integral part of the breech assembly. This permits the fitting of a point sight by a simple slip-on movement, with the sight held in position by pressure.

The new 007 Challenger is well worth a test fire, but those players committed to the original Nel-Spot will welcome the '007' Conversion kit, which allows an easy and inexpensive modification to the New Challenger status.

Full details from: The Nelson Paint Company, P.O. Box 907, Iron Mountain, MI 49801, USA. Tel: (906) 774-5566.

THE SPLATMASTER

The Splatmaster is probably used by most players in their first experience of Paintball. It is an old design but is still the most widely used paint gun in the world.

Constructed from tough plastic, the Splatmaster was advertised as the only 'drip-dry' paintball gun available. It comes in a selection of finishes: green, black or camo, and has developed a reputation for reliability and ease of maintenance; the only metal part being the cocking spring which simply requires an occasional light oiling. The gun is very easy to use and as first-time players can operate it with no problems it is a firm favourite with many sites.

In the basic form the Splatmaster is a .68 inch calibre weapon, with a capacity of 10 rounds internally or up to 18 if the magazine tube is left protruding from the weapon.

American Splatmasters are sold with a muzzle velocity of 230/250fps, but to meet Home Office approval English guns are imported with a muzzle velocity of 170fps. This gives reasonable accuracy up to 70 feet.

Made by National Survival Games and designed to be used by first-timers, the Splatmaster is rugged, but being made of high-impact plastic the gun is very lightweight, tipping the scales at approximately 1.5lb unloaded.

The 12g CO_2 cartridge fits into the pistol grip and is screwed into place by a large black knob. But as more players demand constant air the standard Splatmaster has experienced a number of modifications to its original form. One reason for this is that in the Strathclyde area of Scotland, the police insist that CO_2-powered paintguns are 'firearms' according to the strict letter of the law.

Most other police forces are more tolerant, but to get round this uncertain legality paintball guns in Scotland have been converted to compressed air which places them in the 'air gun' category. The advantage to the player is that most sites provide free air, and 50–60 constant shots can be obtained before the guns need to be recharged.

Early in 1988 the Splatmaster Rapide appeared as a direct successor to the Mk 1 Splatmaster. This smaller gun fires as fast you can pull the trigger, and it delivers more than 20 shots per CO_2 cartridge. Although it was initially slow to take off in the UK Paintball scene, this weapon is now used on many sites throughout the country.

The resin construction of the Rapide is fibre-reinforced, making it strong yet lightweight, and the gun offers tremendous performance and many unique features for an excellent price. Like the Mk 1, the Rapide lends itself readily to customization with up to 50 variants currently available. Its lightweight accuracy and durability makes this weapon an ideal choice.

In mid-1990 the 'Rapide' Competition appeared, looking like something from 'Star Wars'. The Competition has a double-action trigger and offers a high rate of fire but with poor accuracy. The gun comes well supplied with flash suppressor, full grip, 40-round spindle magazine, stock and ring CA adaptor, 7oz tank, pin valve and shoulder sling.

Almost simultaneously, the NSG 'Alligator' was launched and again this is based on the Rapide. It has been adapted to include a custom honed aluminium barrel which accepts a silencer, and a direct feed adaptor enabling you to use either a gravity feed tube, ram box, elbow and ammo box.

For full details on these weapons, contact M.P.I. Limited, Churchgate House, High Street,

▶ *Nelson Quick Splotch — the predecessor of the Nelspot 007.*

▶ *Nel Spot 007 Challenger.*

Edlesborough, Nr Dunstable, Bedfordshire LU6 2LE. Tel: 0525 221395. For information in America call: 800 225 7529, NSG Inc., P.O. Box 1439, New London NH 03257.

CROSMAN .50 REVOLVER

This excellent paintball weapon was available on the UK Paintball scene at the same time as the Splat-

◄ *Basic Splatmaster fitted with focal point sight and constant air tank.*

◄ *Rapide Comp (top), Rapide Alligator (bottom).*

master, and was the site weapon for many early sites. This small gun fires six shots as fast as you can pull the double-action trigger yet it can also be used single action by thumb cocking the hammer for accuracy. The Crosman is intended primarily for short-range shooting at distances of up to 40—45 feet and at these ranges it makes an excellent assault gun and excels in close-combat situations. In 'room

▶ 3357 .50cal Crossman revolver (top), Hideaway snubnose revolver (bottom),

clearing' situations or as a back-up weaon, the Crosman is readily at home because it can be fired quickly with one hand and instant reloading with a six-shot speed loader makes its rate of fire very good.

The Crosman was the first Paintball gun owned by the Author who has fond memories of combat with this little-used weapon. Its main disadvantage is that it fires .50 calibre balls which tend not to impact as well as the larger .62 and .68 calibre. However, much depends on the supplier, make and storage of this size ammo, and it is unreasonable to blame the defect on the weapon.

Noting the popularity of the basic model, The Command Post Inc, have introduced the 'Hideaway'. This is similar to the Model 3357, but has a snub nose barrel and modified hammer. The short, 3-inch barrel gives this gun tremendous manoeuvrability and makes it easy to conceal if you are using it as a back-up gun, much to the surprise of your opponents. As always, however, check that the site on which you are playing allows this before carrying a back-up.

On test, the Author obtained 30–35 shots per CO_2 bulb, although it will vary widely depending on the brand of CO_2 cartridge. This Enfield-style break-front revolver sits well in the hand and still has élitist supporters who love the looks and feel of the weapon.

The Crosman 3357 is a paintball spin-off from the Crosman 38 target revolver, which was a six-shot .177 CO_2-powered air pistol that was very popular in the States at the beginning of the eighties, but never succeeded in the UK because of the firearms law on gas-powered air pistols.

Further details from: Crosman Air Guns, Routes 5 & 20, East Bloomfield, New York 14443, USA.

STANDARD NIGHTMARE

The Nightmare .68 calibre pump-action paint gun is attractively finished owing to its extruded anodised aluminium construction. An added attraction is the easy to attach shoulder stock supplied so that the gun can be used as a pistol or as a rifle. Easily converted to constant air, the Nightmare was the basis for the 'Ninja' series. The standard Nightmare gives 20–25 shots per CO_2 cartridge and changing is simply achieved by turning a large knurled bolt, tipping out the spent bulb and replacing it with a new one: easily done in under five seconds.

At the start of the Paintball boom, the standard Nightmare became very popular with those players who liked to pump a lot of paint. If the pump is operated with the trigger held in, the weapon will fire on each return stroke, and with practise the fire rate is almost as good as a semi-automatic. Weighing in at about 3.5 pounds, the gun is easiest to handle with a stock fitted; some players find it too heavy for one-handed use.

The standard model was soon replaced by the Nightmare gravity feed, which could accommodate an ammo drum and was far better than the 10-ball magazine.

The early standard Nightmare is rarely seen now, the manufacturers, Brass Eagle Inc., having numerous hi-tech weapons rolling out of their plant in Ontario. The new Cobra, King Cobra, semi-automatic Jaguar, and semi-automatic Barracuda DMR-40 are some of the most technically advanced guns available direct from the factory.

For details contact: Brass Eagle Inc., 7050-A Bramalea Road, Unit 19, Mississauga, Ontario L5S 1T1 Canada. Tel: (416) 848-4844.

SHERIDAN PGP

This Paintball weapon is named after a 'street sign' and Sheridan are one of the best-known manufac-turers in America. Sheridan air rifles and Paintball weapons do not carry the name of their inventor as Sheridan air weaponry traces its origins to Racine, Wisconsin. There, in 1945, E. N. Wackerhagen saw a large potential for the superior grade of pneumatic rifle, and enlisted the engineering and mechanical co-operation of Bob Kraus.

After the American Civil War, a major highway linked Chicago, Illinois, and Green Bay, Wisconsin and was known as Sheridan Road. The road served Racine as the city's South Main Street. With develop-ment of the prototype nearly completed, the gun was still unnamed until both realized that they lived on the same street, and thus named it Sheridan.

The Sheridan paintgun is based on a CO_2-powered air pistol and was made of steel and alloy with an overall black finish. The weight of 2.5 pounds makes the PGP well balanced and a comfortable gun to hold, but changing the CO_2 cartridges is slightly awkward: unscrew the knurled end cap, remove complete with plunger, tip out the old cartridge. To replace new CO_2 cartridge repeat process in reverse.

Loading the paintballs is far easier. Take the end cap off the magazine and tip in a full tube of balls. With a ball in the breech the gun holds 10 balls although an ammo tube left slotted in the magazine would increase capacity significantly. The PGP was one of the first weapons to be customized, and

▲ *The basic Nightmare.*

◄ *Sheridan PGP.*

perhaps the first in the UK to include constant air tanks. This was one of the first Constant Air weapons used by the Author when introduced into Britain by Mayhem. Sheridan have since expanded to produce new weapons, well advanced from the first PGP pistol.

For details of the new range of Sheridan weaponry contact: Pursuit Marketing Inc. (USA). Tel: 312/272 4765.

CUSTOM SHERIDAN PGP

This gun has become the standard for quality, accuracy and power, by which many players judge other paintball guns. In its standard form the PGP is compact, accurate and provides ample power and range, but by adding some performance accessories this gun can be transformed from a standard site gun to a formidable piece of hardware.

▲ Custom PGP.

The customized PGP as illustrated features a combat Delrin pump and a custom fit Crosman stock with constant air bottle holder installed. All metal parts are satin nickel plated which gives great durability and ease of cleaning, but does tend to reflect the sun.

As well as coming with functional hose armour, the installation of a Sheridan pistol speed loader increases magazine capacity to 20 rounds. This is obviously a highly versatile gun, capable even of tournament use at the time it was in fashion. An enormous assortment of accessories is still available, which makes the PGP a contender as the basis of a weapons system.

THE EXCALIBUR

This British-made weapon is one of a series designed around 'The Phantom', with priorities being cost and reliability. The barrel is 8 inches long and is made of high-grade honed aluminium. All the internals, hammer, bolt, springs, valve stem and seat, are made of stainless steel. Options include a variety of colour finishes and a stock to transform the piece into a rifle. On test the Excalibur was extremely accurate and very robust for its size and weight.

The Excalibur's size and compact design make it very 'user-friendly' and the embossed finish to the pump and pistol grips adds an extra touch of style to the overall appearance of a fine weapon that is good to use and available at a modest price.

For full details contact: N.W.C. Paintball Limited, Unit 20, Burnham Trading Estate, Burnham Road, Dartford, Kent DA1 5BH. Tel: 9322 222270.

PRO-SERIES TOURNAMENT GUNS

All Pro-Series guns feature the new, tournament length weld-less barrel assembly, and these beautifully finished, distortion-free barrels make for a lightweight and remarkably accurate weapon. The guns also feature the new smooth Delrin pump assembly, and the bolt, sere and valve assembly have been reworked to assure smooth operation, rapid feeding, and maximum legal velocity. A dove-tail mounting base is provided as standard, and the barrel will accept a silencer. The Pro-Tournament series comprises a number of different guns that are

▶ *Excalibur.*

▼ *Pro-Tournament series.*

of the latest direct-feed design and that will accept a variety of different loaders.

The Author owns this system and for fast movement and substantial hitting power uses the Pro-Tournament Mk 5. This offers all the features of the standard guns, but has a Micro CA Instant CO_2 Quick Change Combat Stock. This ingenious device not only allows for instant 'fall-in-fall-out' of CO_2 bulbs (2 seconds), but also incorporates a one-way internal gas valve which will allow the gun to fire once or twice even with the CO_2 bulb removed, giving a useful tactical advantage. A further advantage is that you can screw the Micro CA unit out and quickly change over to the larger constant air tanks.

The Mk 5 thus offers excellent performance together with enormous versatility. An alternative is the Pro-Sport Mk 2 which is fine when the game gets a little more serious because a 10oz bottle can be fitted to the bottle-holder stock. This system utilizes rear entry constant air and is very handy when combat becomes tough. When fitted with a silencer it is very imposing, giving a deadly combination of firepower, accuracy and versatility.

The Pro-Tournament-Sport Series is clearly one of the most versatile systems available with good personal customization capacity.

APEX ELITE

Air Power of Norfolk, Virginia now manufacture their own gun, the Apex Elite. Taking all the refinements of their Nel-Spot conversion kit and combining them with a new M-16-style pistol grip results in a fast handling, smooth cocking, accurate shooting paint gun.

The major features of the Elite are its forward-drop feeding system, self-centering hammer/bolt, and venturi bolt face. The forward drop chambers a ball directly into the bore thus reducing the chances of pinching a ball while cocking. The self-centering hammer/bolt system makes pumping much smoother, and the venturi bolt, combined with the unique 12-inch barrel, produces excellent accuracy

and range. The pistol grip assembly also has note-worthy features: if the trigger is held back the gun will fire as soon as the bolt closes, and the trigger is adjustable for take-up and over travel. The internal power components are designed for maximum performance and there is even a shock absorber built into the pump bolt to cut down on metal to metal wear.

Air Power produces every part used in this weapon so all the components fit and function excellently, and it has an enviable reputation for reliability — so much so that the Apex Elite was selected by the US Marine Corps as the paint weapon for use in its training programme.

Specifications
Calibre: .68.
Barrel length: 7 or 12 inches.
Overall length: 31 inches with a 12-inch barrel and 7oz constant air tank.
Weight: 31lb 4oz without constant air tank.
Manufacturer: Air Power, 7425 Sewells Point Road, Ste.E Norfolk, VA 23513 USA.

▼ *Apex Elite.*

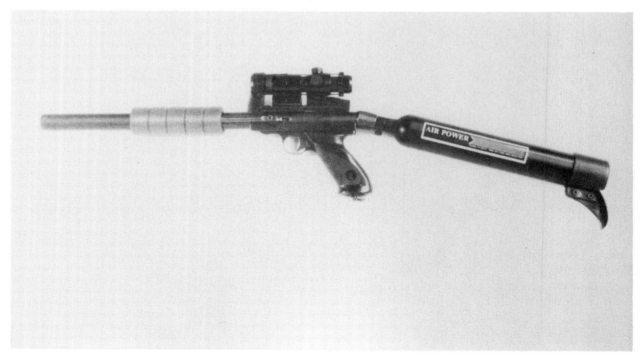

'REB LINE' TOURNAMENT GUN

The Reb Line is unique in that it was produced for the 'serious' Paintball player, but closer examination uncovers five Paintball firsts:

1 A specially built tight bore barrel reduces spin and gives deadly accuracy. The gun is also equipped with collar feed and troy gold brass knurled thumbscrew to hold the gravity feed in place.

2 A 'quick-change pump' snaps on and off with just the pressure of two fingers without the need to remove the bolt knobs. The pump is almost a full inch longer than the standard wrap-around pump and it can accommodate large hands as well as small. This can be bought separately and fits 99 per cent of all dual-armed wrap-around pump guns.

3 Adjustable screw in valve body. The Allen head post adjusts for almost any depth of pin valve bottle or quick change, and a bleed hole is incorporated to avoid the chance of damage to 'O' rings during bottle change; a safety feature in case your pin thermo valve breaks.

4 An M-16 style dove-tail sight adjustable for different ranges.

5 An interchangeable screw-in Delrin bolt with self-lubricating brass base. Four patterns are available so that one can select the best one for the situation, such as temperature or type of paint. Four styles of bolt are available, although the gun is fitted with the 'inverted volcano' pattern as standard.

There are so many excellent features on this gun that it is difficult to list them all: no friction because of the self-lubricating anti-kink brass bolt and hammer; drop bore system barrel; all the screws are made in troy gold brass and knurled. Reb Line tight bore guns can be cleaned, including the complete bolt area, bolt and barrel, in less than twenty seconds.

All external parts are made from finest aluminium and the guns are available in the following colours: black, red, grey, burgundy, wine, deep purple, forest green, royal blue and troy gold.

For full details contact: Confederate Army Supply Line, 9810 Owensmouth, Suite 8, Chatsworth, CA 91311, USA. Tel: (818) 998 1862.

NATIONAL GUN SPORTS 'SAVAGE'

The new model is intended for those who want a paint gun suitable both for the rough and tumble of normal games and the critical performance demanded in competitions. National Gun Sports spent the majority of the development of this gun in refining the barrel length, bore and finish to achieve the final

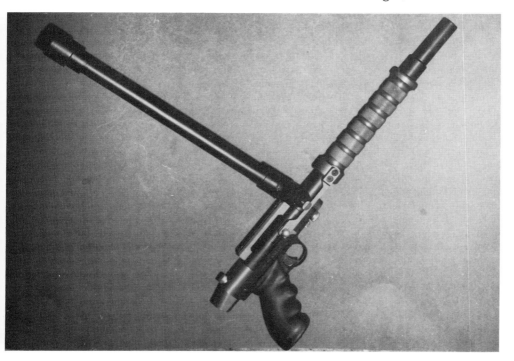

◄ *Reb Line.*

specification requirements they had established.

G. M. 'Kes' Kessler as President of National Gun Sports Corporation obviously sets a very high standard for the weapons that NGS produces. With a BSc in Electrical Engineering at the Florida Institute of Technology, Kes has worked in research and development engineering for 24 years. From 1962 to 1969 his involvement at Cape Kennedy included the Gemini and Apollo space projects as well as the Poseidon Programme. After involvement with NASA, the US Army and the US Navy, he became a consultant in satellite navigation systems for shipping fleets.

A change came in 1986 with his decision to work at what he enjoyed. A keen Paintball enthusiast since 1977, he began to view Paintball in a new light and decided that, 'An overwhelming problem with much Paintball equipment has been a preponderance of junk offered to players. For extremely handsome prices, you can purchase more garbage in Paintball than just about any other endeavour.'

His views were reflected by the National Gun Sports Corporation, dedicated to the production of quality products. With his engineering background and the considerable talents of his master machinist, Robert Mannus, he began developing components for after market application. Output quickly grew to the vast range of products that NGS supply to the industry today.

As the flagship of the NGS production line, the 'Savage' Mk 1 was the result of some five months of tests and refinement, succeeded only in the nineties by the Mk 2. Before starting production of the Savage, NGS reviewed the weaponry available at the time and found that no single piece included all the features needed by players. These were identified as:

1 40 to 50 yards' range.
2 Accurate enough to hit a man-sized target at these ranges.
3 Light.
4 Reliable.
5 Quick and easy to field strip and clean.
6 Durable.
7 Quick firing.
8 Simple in design and construction.

The most challenging of these requirements were the range and accuracy demands so most of the development period was spent on refining barrel length, bore diameter and finish, to achieve the specification.

The lightness and durability of the Savage is attributable to the selection of 6061 aluminium as the principal material. When anodized, this metal is tough, durable, corrosion resistant and very stable in almost all weather conditions. Due to the unique two thumbscrews the Savage can be field stripped in seconds. The author has seen Kes strip a Savage in

◀ *Savage.*

eleven seconds without any tools, and reassemble almost as quickly. This is particularly important since maintenance is often neglected on the more complicated guns. The old engineering phrase 'K.I.S.S. – Keep It Simple Stupid' evolved from the fact that, inevitably, reliability and simplicity are complementary, and the Savage is a tribute to such ultimate simplicity with only three moving parts.

The Mk 1 Savage of .62 calibre went on sale in the UK in 1988, although the market was not quite ready for it. In 1990 the NGS Savage Mk 2 was introduced with better response. As the Mk 1 was based on the 'Nel-Spot', the Mk 2 is still quite modest in external appearance except that it now has a single-rail wrap-around pump, plus the same Lone Star receiver as used on the Bushmaster Deluxe. A particularly impressive aspect of the Mk 2 is the bolt and hammer system. The hammer is now of self-lubricating brass and the bolt is very similar to that found on the Phantom, except that it has a long extended sleeve to avoid spring-kink and to reduce wear on the housing.

The Mk 2 Savage is also particularly impressive when used on site: for the author shot a full hopper of 40 rounds without a single break and hit the target 36 times at 30 yards. When used with the auto-trigger another two full hoppers passed through the gun without any problems.

Further details from the manufacturer: The National Gun Sports Corporation, PO Drawer 290, ARK, Virginia 23003, USA.

TIPPMAN-SMG-60

This exciting and unique .62 calibre gun has its own 250–300 shot constant air system built in, and features a 15-shot magazine which loads three 5-shot paintball holders or 'stripper clips'. These stripper clips are automatically ejected from the gun every fifth shot. The American version of the SMG-60 will fire full auto at approximately 600 rounds per minute, but the version for the British market will fire semi-auto only. The SMG-60 is an accurate and powerful gun capable of great firepower, but does require more attention to detail and proper maintenance than other paintball guns. This is one of the factors that gave owners 'teething problems', because like most modern semi-autos proper maintenance is vital.

The basic range has increased substantially since its first appearance in 1988 and now includes: SMG Basic, SMG Bulldog, SMG Sniper and SMG-60 Custom (fitted with scope, silencer, clip-catcher, bipod and new high feed system).

When the first SMG-60 arrived in the UK there was uncertainty as to how legal it was to own a CO_2 weapon of this type and style. Despite rumours to the contrary, the gun was classed as an 'air gun', and provided that it meets the requirements of ownership and use normally applied to air guns it does not need a licence. The air cylinder is easy to recharge from a standard diver's bottle, available from your local Paintball shop or BOC.

In the UK during the late eighties, the SMG used compressed air and not CO_2 like the American version. The advantage is that compressed air is cheap, and a full diving cylinder will provide many refills to the gun's reservoir. On first firing the SMG-60 you will find the semi-automatic mode a great experience as it simulates the actual firing of an automatic centre-fire firearm with blow-back bolt system. The weight of 5 pounds also gives the SMG-60 just the right feel. The gun's strength and durability derives from its construction from high grade aluminium and stainless steel.

SMGs in use today are mostly CO_2 powered and in .62 and .68 calibre, and on site the Bulldog SMG is an easy weapon to use. This weapon is a real 'beast' and a Paintball manufacturer's dream. The semi-automatic fire is so exhilarating that it is all too easy to fire five or six hundred balls in under half an hour.

The Bulldog has a short, assault-length barrel with a 3.5oz CO_2 bottle, which makes it an ideal close-combat weapon. This model also comes with 10-round speed clips for faster reloading and will accept 10-, 15-, or 20-round magazines. The author prefers the 'flip 15' speed clips which provide 30

rounds of firepower in mere seconds. The grooved receiver is designed for the fitting of a Daisy Point sight or a full scope.

The Tippman SMGs reception on UK sites has been mixed, but the SMG-60 has blasted its way into Paintball history and will remain a potent weapon for some time.

Further details from: Tippman Pneumatics Inc., 4402 New Haven Avenue, Fort Wayne, Indiana 46803, USA.

THE SL .68 (SABRE)

The SL .68 body is cast as a single piece of hard magnesium/aluminium, thus doing away with the need for more twenty other parts. The slot removed from the breech serves two functions: for cleaning the weapon should the barrel be painted and using the pull-through fed through the breech and away from the bolt face. The slot also allows full viewing of the loading process. The .68 barrel is a good fit to the breech with exact internal diameters and although the ball travels from breech to barrel it doesn't suffer any change of diameter — often the primary cause of ball breakage.

◀ *SL 68 Sabre.*

Dismantling the SL .68 involves releasing a single Allen bolt at the front of the body and once loosened, the 11-inch aluminium barrel slides clear. By giving the pump handle a tug the bolt is dislodged. A slight tap will then release the hammer assembly leaving the power stem, which is removed by un-screwing the two Allen bolts at the rear of the body. The internal parts of the SL .68 are made of stainless steel.

TIPPMAN 68 SPECIAL SEMI-AUTOMATIC

The new semi from Tippman's range arrived just too late to include a full product report.

The 68 Special is a new hybrid weapon with proven Tippman quality and reliability. Combining the ruggedness of the SL.68 and the speed of the SMG-60, the 68 Special is a true semi-automatic and not a double-action.

With a new gravity feed system that helps eliminate ball breakage and double feeding, the 68 Special has a light trigger movement which allows a very high rate of fire and a new liquid CO_2 system gives up to 200 rapid shots per fill without loss of velocity.

For full details contact: Tippman Pneumatics Inc., 4402 New Haven Avenue, Fort Wayne, Indiana 46803, USA. Tel: 219/422 6448.

THE RAZORBACK

This fine Paintball weapon has a unique history and merits a book in its own right. Here are the facts that make this weapon legendary.

The Razorback is loosely an embryo of the Nel-Spot 007 pistol and the trigger housing is similar to the Phantom at first glance. But on closer inspection the Razorback's housing has a very fine finish with much crisper lines. Every surface is finished to a high standard with no sharp edges and the trigger guard is more comfortable than one usually finds. The trigger is just right and the housing contains a full power auto-trigger as standard. The housing is attached to the barrel and quick-change unit by two stainless steel field strip bolts.

It is easy to see in the Razorback features similar to other weaponry; for example, when stripping the weapon the similarity to a Bushmaster becomes apparent. But the Razorback is the ultimate refinement of features from the very best weaponry.

The bolt is cast and polished in solid stainless steel and an 'O' ring is fitted to the end of the bolt to

► *68 Special semi-automatic.*

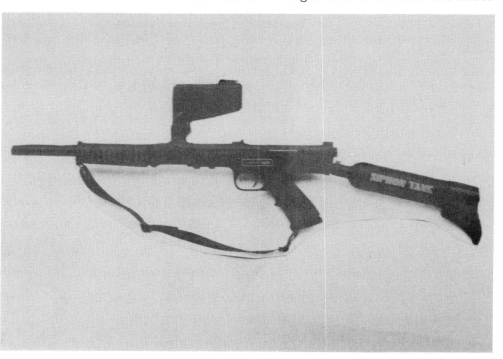

▲ *Razorback.*

make a positive leak-free fit. An inspection of the hammer reveals one of the most hi-tech items currently fitted to a box standard weapon. Unlike the Bushmaster hammer, which has the anti-binding step built in, the hammer on the Razorback has two wide slots to minimize friction and due to excellent machining these create very close tolerances and very precise alignment. The site production models are still matching the original high standard.

The anodizing on the weapon is hard and not merely cosmetic as you find on the aluminium of second-rate weaponry. The Razorback comes with 11-inch and 14-inch helix barrels with muzzle brakes built in, and the standard basic version is available with an 11-inch smooth bore barrel.

Specifications:

Calibre: 0.68 inch.

Feed System: gravity feed, bore drop.

Action: single-stroke pump.

Power: CO_2 or Constant Air.

Weight: 2lb.

For full UK details contact: Ultimate Game, Adams Fruit Farm, Ivy House Lane, Hastings, East Sussex TN35 4NN. Tel: 0424 753588.

THE BLACK WIDOW

The very latest paintgun from the Ultimate Game stable, the Black Widow is available as either a fixed-barrel gun or, as in the de luxe version, boasting three interchangeable barrels, supplied as standard, micro-bored to 8-inch, 10.5-inch or 14-inch specification. The Black Widow has newly developed grips for extra comfort and better handling, and easy field-strippable steel-lined screw holes. To field strip fully requires the removal of four screws. Other features include dual-rail bind-free pump and bolt system; stainless steel internals and the trigger is fully adjustable to permit full slam fire as well as single shot. The Black Widow comes fitted with a quick change 12gr with capacity for constant air.

Ultimate Game have always led the field by supplying the very best in Paintball weaponry and the Black Widow appears well set to dominate the market.

For full details contact: Ultimate Game, Mail Order Wholesale Retail Export, UK–Europe–USA, Adams Fruit Farm, Ivy House Lane, Hastings, East Sussex TN35 4NN. Tel: 0424 753588.

THE EDGE

The Edge was first produced in America under the name of the 'Equaliser' and manufactured by Cross-

▲ *Black Widow.*

► *The Edge.*

fire. However the Equaliser never appeared following an unexplained chain of events. In August 1989 Larry Littlefield saw the potential of the weapon and tried to produce the 'Edge' for both the UK and American markets.

The Author was privileged to be the first UK journalist to test and photograph the Edge and was amazed by its features; there was nothing on the Paintball scene to match it. The Edge has more than a passing resemblance to the weapons used by anti-terrorist units as there are no ammo tubes or hopper boxes sticking out of this weapon. The magazine is within the stock and has capacity for 22 rounds, plus an extra 38 from a clip-on accessory magazine. This

is a unique feature as the balls are fed into the breech by a constant tension spring.

Loading is simplicity itself; one merely feeds the balls through the side port at the rear of the weapon. Once full, pulling the knob at the centre of the feed block towards you and pushing it back in behind the last ball constantly feeds the balls into the breech every time the trigger is pulled. The magazine feed is extremely smooth because even pressure is applied to the rounds from the first to the last shot. An open slot runs the full length of the magazine enabling the player to assess at a glance how much ammo remains, particularly useful in the midst of a heavy fire fight.

The Edge has a triple port venturi bolt, but most weapons on the Paintball scene have a single port which expels the gas/air directly on to the ball. This often causes ball breakage because the gas hits the ball in one spot and a soft or thin ball will burst under pressure. This is impossible with the Edge as the three ports are directed towards the barrel side. A further advantage of this method is that the gas fills the space behind the ball with an even pressure as it fires the ball down the barrel.

In standard mode the Edge is powered by two CO_2 cartridges inserted into the pistol grip, but there is the option of a constant air cylinder fitted under the magazine. The shoulder stock extends to fit any user and gives an overall compact feel to the weapon.

If you should by unlucky chance have a paintball break in the barrel, the Edge opens like a conventional shotgun and the barrel can be cleaned immediately. When tested by Ray Cain, the Paintball photographer and weaponry expert for Paintball Games Magazine UK, the Edge fired 4,000 paintballs without a single breakage. The Author's own test revealed no faults at all, even when used with low quality paintballs to try and force a breakage.

Non-weapon related problems however have confined the Edge only to a very lucky few in the UK, but in late 1990 the Edge returned to the UK and European markets. The weapon now has another name and is sold as the BE 90, manufactured by the China State Owned Qianjin Arsenal, PRC and supplied via: Major Paintball Industries, 16 Slicketts Lane, Edlesborough, Bedfordshire LU6 2JD. Tel: 0525 221395.

PMI PIRANHA

PMI produce two versions of the Piranha: with a short or with a long barrel, and that is the only difference between them. Both weapons have the same receiver, valve, bolt and power source. Fitted with a speed demon centrefire bolt the weapon has speed and a smooth action. A bonus is that bolts can be field stripped without the need for tools. Both Piranhas have the same receiver and can be powered via a donkey that will accept constant air in a 3.5oz bottle for the short barrel, or 7oz bottle for the long barrel. A choice of power supply means the Piranhas can take a Six-Pack, Micro CA, Rat Attack, or any of the range of power supply accessories available including the 'Turbovalve' which has improved the CO_2 consumption of the gun.

Although available in the UK only since 1989, the Piranha has a pedigree of nine years and its popularity will ensure its survival for years to come.

For details in UK, contact: Mayhem Paintball Games Ltd, Sunset Farm, Cross In Hand, Heathfield, East Sussex. In the USA: Pursuit Marketing Inc., 1980 Raymond Drive, Northbrook IL 60062, USA.

PIRANHA RIFLE

PMI have also released a new rifle in the Piranha Series, called the KP3. It boasts a 50-round ammo box which feeds paintballs into the barrel through a

► PMI Pirahna.

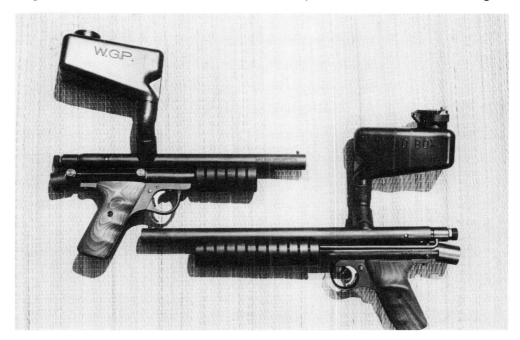

▼ Pirahna Rifle.

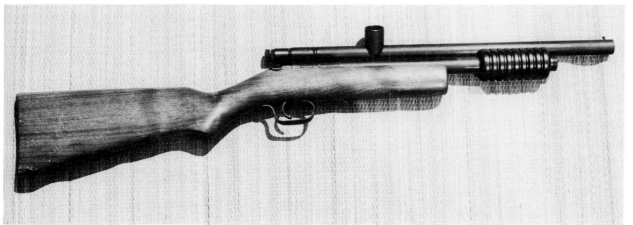

brass direct-feed elbow. The elbow is solidly brazed to the barrel and this direct-feed system eliminates the need to tilt the gun in order to chamber a round. The feed elbow is also notched and thus forms the rear sight of the new peep sight system. CO_2 is supplied by a 7oz constant air tank, located in a carrier beneath the gun, which feeds the gas through a braided stainless steel hose to the front of the lower barrel. The constant air supply gives the rifle a highly accurate and consistent fire pattern. PMI's new Speed Demon bolt, standard in all of their new Piranha Series models, is also included in the KP3 Piranha rifle. The design of this bolt causes the outward pressure on the detent system to be released during the initial movement of the pump, and a spring-loaded cocking lug allows the bolt to be field stripped without any tools.

Supply details are as for other PMI products.

PMI SEMI-AUTO

This new weapon from the PMI stable appeared just as this book was about to go to press, so details are limited, but there is a photograph to show this new weapon off.

The gun features a blow-back semi-automatic mechanism with a crisp, short trigger pull and each weapon comes with:
One removable barrel.
One ammo box (without cover).
One constant air tank.
One velocity adjustment tool.

The shoulder stock is optional and all other options in the photograph are sold separately.

For full details of dealers contact: Pursuit Marketing Inc., 1980 Raymond Drive, Northbrook, IL 60062, USA. Tel: 708 272 4765.

For details in Canada: 875 Foster Avenue, Suite 107, Windsor, Ontario, Canada N8X 4W3. Tel: 519 972 5440.

▼ *Pirahna System.*

▲ *PMI Semi-Auto.*

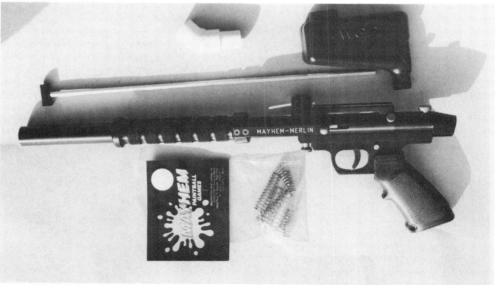

▶ *Mayhem
Merlin.*

MAYHEM MERLIN

The current Mayhem weapon on the market is actually American, but sold under their own name: The Merlin. The weapon has a trigger/grip unit produced by the American Wintec Co., and is a nice piece of equipment, the pistol grip being fully adjustable so that the player can set it to suit his hand. The trigger is a straight pull type with adjustable sear and length of pull, and the Merlin comes with 11-inch or 14-inch barrels. The pump is twin-sided and attached by twin brass rod-bolts, and with a donkey as standard. A nice point is that the donkey is fitted with twin gas transfer ports and a fully length adjustable centre pin.

A Mayhem test gave 38 to 42 shots per 12gram CO_2 cylinder, which shows that the modern weapon is more efficient in gas consumption than weapons of only two years ago. The trigger on the Merlin can be locked over to give permanent slam-fire, but it can be quickly re-set to single fire by pushing the safety back which sets the trigger to single fire mode.

Specifications:

Barrel length: 11 inch or 14 inch fixed.

Trigger: Single-shot or slam-fire with slam-fire lock-out.

Weight: 2lb (14-inch barrel, no gas system).

Safety: Cross bolt.

Pump stroke: 1 inch.

For full details contact Mayhem Paintball Games Ltd., Tel: 04352 6189/5612.

MAD-MAX

The 'Mad-Max' is a Command Post Inc., custom gun based on the Sheridan rifle and is ideal for those players who wish to be the centre of attention before the game has begun. It is a truly compact assault-type gun which offers maximum fire power, and the provision of a muzzle flash suppressor, point sight and short hand grip stock proves that this is a serious weapon. To increase the fire rate the gun has a direct feed system, and the extra-long combat pump supplied gives a better gripping surface than normal which allows for a more responsive rapid-fire action. For those used to the normal early Sheridan pump rifle with 10-shot magazine and 10 or 12 full power shots from one charge, the 'Mad-Max' will come as a nice surprise.

This weapon provides 150 rounds plus capability from its 3.5oz constant air system, and a short tube magazine rather than the box hopper improves the assault image of the weapon. The Author has played with team mates who own the 'Max-Max' and who have fitted a drum gravity feeder giving 120+ rounds at one load, and find the weapon handles superbly. As with all forms of custom weaponry you either love it or hate it and after using the 'Mad-Max' the Author is firmly in the first camp.

▼ *Sheridan Mad-Max constant air weapon.*

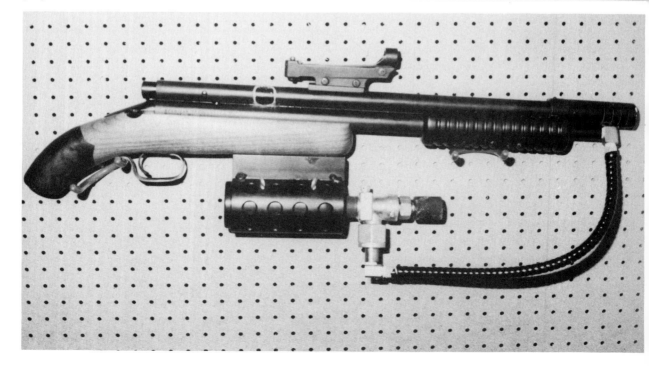

THE PHANTOM

Well proven at tournament level, this weapon demands the attention of any serious player. The Phantom has a 10.5-inch aluminium roller burnished barrel (a superior process that delivers a smoother, harder barrel lining) topped with a gold-plated front sight post. For maximum speed, the 5-inch raised rib Delrin pump makes cocking almost effortless as the capture short-stroke cocking system and bolt design give silky smooth cocking action with very little possibility of jamming.

The unique gravity feed system of the Phantom is based around the screw-in drop tube, secured by a locknut. The sleek tapered barrel design gives a total weight of only 1.9 pounds, and a hard anodized finish both improves the appearance of this gun as well as providing long-lasting durability. To enable a point sight or scope to be fitted the Phantom comes equipped with low profile 'V'-grooved sight rail.

To speed up CO_2 changes there is the rear quick-change system. All internal parts are nickel plated for corrosion-free, low maintenance performance. The seal material was purposely developed for CO_2 and will cost you pennies rather than pounds when you need to replace it.

The power tube is stainless steel and of a similar basic design to the Nel-Spot but with one or two changes: they are not interchangeable and there are three angled holes instead of two straight holes and the stroke is shorter.

When fully loaded with 20 rounds and gas the Phantom weighs 2.25 pounds, but with a length of 20 inches the Phantom is still a light and user-friendly weapon.

Accessories for the Phantom include various constant air systems, different ammo boxes, bulk hoppers, stick feeds and silencers. Straight from the box, this is one gun that out-performs its advertising hype.

For the full range of Phantoms, plus unique one-off custom weapons, contact: Pro Player Products, R & R Paintball, Unit D10, Seedbed Centre, Rom Valley Way, Romford, Essex. Tel: 0708 740387.

THE TERRIER

This is another new breed of Paintball weapon that at first glance looks like a Phantom. Made by the

▼ *Phantom.*

Precision Machine Company of Wiltshire, the Terrier comes with a 'Lone Star' grip, breech drop, and gravity feed loading system. The standard weapon comes with a 10.5-inch barrel made of high grade aluminium and the weapon's internals are made of top quality stainless steel. The anti-kink bolt, hammer and power tube are all very much the same as on the Phantom, but the Terrier is far easier on the pocket. The price of the Terrier in no way reflects the finish of the weapon as all the internals are well finished and highly polished. The barrels are anodized to a good hard even finish in black, but a choice of red, blue, green and gold is available.

The Precision Machine Company also produce a tournament version with a 12-inch barrel with dial-a-bolt, dial-a-rod, sight rail and trigger shoe for a slightly higher price.

The gas chamber takes a little getting used to because you have to unscrew the end plug fully before you can change the gas, but with practise this becomes user-friendly. The pump-action cocking is light and easy to use and has a relatively short stroke.

To strip the Terrier, just two screws hold the barrel and grip and removing the front screw, pulling the barrel out and twisting to free from the pump grip completes the entire stripping process.

The Terrier stands up to hard use and action of the rough novice and still looks good as barrel inspection from random sites showed the internals to look as new. With the option of barrels at 10.5-, 12-, 14-, and 16-inches and soon a new hi-tech carbon-fibre barrel, the Terrier is one of the new versatile British weapons.

Full details from: Action Pursuit Centre, Croxely Green, Hertfordshire. Tel: 0923 897090.

THE BUSHMASTER

The Bushmaster (t.m.) SI Tournament Series, is manufactured by Skirmish of California and the weapon reviewed here is the Bushmaster 90, owned by Robert Newby of Bad Company, London, England.

This weapon has a custom 45 grip, Pachmayer combat grips, and Bottom Line by Lapco. A six pack is added to the bottom line with a bottom line to the donkey. A Pointman pump and barrel combine to make this a great weapon.

The forward drop bolt system chambers the ball directly into the bore and so the bolt does not have to push the next ball back into the feeder, thereby eliminating the clipping found on standard breech-

▲ *Bushmaster.*

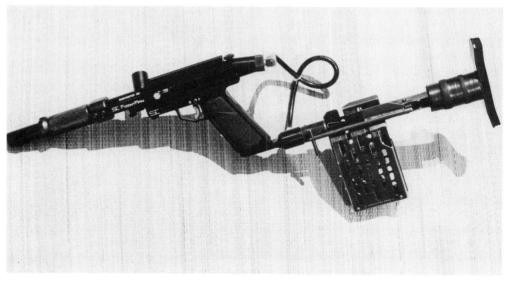

▶ *Bushmaster.*

drop type guns. The bolt allows for good expansion of the gas and is made out of Delrin and aluminium, which gives super-smooth pumping.

The 'Six-Pack' fitted was seen for the first time at the Nashville International in October 1989. This is a device that will boost the rate of fire by reducing the time it takes to change a gas cartridge. The Six Pack is loaded in the same way as you would load bullets into a rifle or pistol magazine.

In use, once the first gas cartridge is empty you pull back the lever which jettisons the old CO_2 cartridge. A fresh cartridge is pushed into place as you return the lever forwards.

The Six Pack adds extra weight to the Bushmaster 90 (about 2 pounds unloaded, and 2lb 8oz loaded), but combined with the Pointman system it makes a great tournament weapon.

For details of the Bushmaster (t.m) SI Tournament Series USA contact: (818) 705 6615 for Line SI Dealer nearest you.

Python.

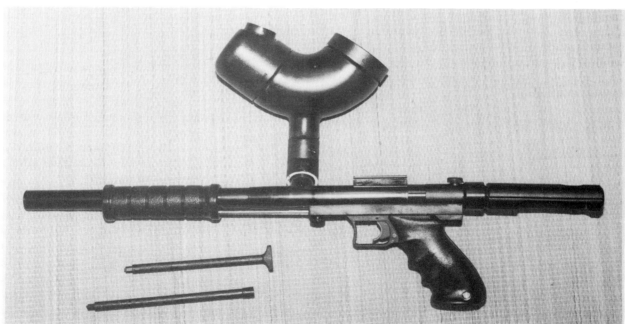

▼ *Viper.*

THE PYTHON AND VIPER

When Paintball was young, most players used the Splatmaster, the first 'Drip-Dry' paint gun.

The Splat had only one metal part, the cocking spring, and most current players used this plastic gun without flinching at its plastic construction. The Splatmaster is still the world's most used paint weapon. It is strange then that when a plastic-based weapon appears it is instantly criticized for being made of plastic. Bernie Frier of Hi-Tech Industries has been in the gun and Paintball trade since the start. Hi-Tech produce two guns that are Britain's first home-grown plastic weaponry: the Python and Viper. When interviewed about plastic he replied: 'Plastic is a good medium. Give me any reason why a paintgun has got to be metal. I know at the very start we had one or two teething problems, which certain sectors of the industry still try to use to verbally smash our products.'

As many as 80 per cent of the steel guns on the market are made from poor alloy, but now players are beginning to accept that a good paint gun can be made from plastic. Both the Python and the Viper have metal components within the weapons and the barrel on the Python is brass. 'We can do a far higher ultra-mirror finish with plastic, but we would have so much customer resistance if we tried to market the all-plastic barrel, but there is no reason at all why the plastic barrel should not be excepted. It has taken over two years to get to the point where we are today, it has cost us over half a million in development costs to replicate the all-steel Nel-Spot in plastic. But now, we have produced the Python and Viper in a space age material called Nylafil.' This new plastic/glass material has super strength and durability, and is not affected by corrosion, rust and abrasion.

The original concept came at a bad time for the company because producing a plastic Nel-Spot was a very hard task. 'I'm sure we could have made our self-designed plastic gun for a fraction of the cost, but we finally came up with the right formula, which is what you see on the production lines of our factory today.' When in full production, 500–700 guns come out of the factory each week, in fact Bernie confided that: 'We just can't make enough to keep up with our order book.' Hi-Tech have just scooped a massive order from an American Company, making an all time first for the UK Paintball Industry by actually exporting British weaponry to the States. This is a seal of approval for Hi-Tech and the turning-point in the acceptance of a British plastic paint weapon.

The factory at Erith in Kent is a hive of activity as every item for the Viper and Python is made by Hi-Tech. The process starts with a sack of plastic granules and through a chain of custom-built plastic extrusion machines and state-of-the-art mouldings the weapon takes form.

The small production and technical staff have substantial expertise, having followed an idea into reality. As a result loyalty and dedication are obvious at every stage of the weapon. With a machine turning out a trigger sear every one and a half seconds, the time in development is now paying off. Technicians work on machines that hone the barrels while others test each weapon before it is made ready for packaging, and this lead to a very high degree of quality control. The company is keen to keep their weapons to a realistic price; for example, after the plastic moulding and extrusion processes have been completed, the 'swarf' waste plastic is collected and reground to be used again, so the total wastage is only 1 per cent of all materials.

The Python and Viper are both exported worldwide, but Europe remains the biggest sales market. Speculation has it that Germany and France are going to be the world's largest consumers this decade, so a new company has been set up in Belgium. There is certainly a place for the plastic paintball weapon on the world market, and Hi-Tech Industries is making a real effort to become established as the foremost supplier.

The Python comes complete with the classic HT speed change, full round dynamic pump power, adjustable bolt, custom grips, 8-inch removable brass barrel and universal ammo feeder accepting 10-shot tubes or 45-shot hoppers. Also fitted as standard is the revolutionary HT power system; a totally new concept of power management. The Python has open combat sights plus an optical sight fitting rail. The overall length is 45cm; weight 825g.

The Viper must be the cheapest tournament-capable gun available, with 8-inch speedball barrel and 11-inch 'Tourney' barrel. Each Viper comes with an extra power tube, two spare cup seals and a comprehensive manual.

Full details from: Hi-Tech Industries (UK) Ltd., 23–25 Kencot Way, Yarnton Way, Erith, Kent DA18 4AE. Tel: 081 312 1989.

WGP RANGER

The Ranger has been designed to remain in touch with the changing face of Paintball weaponry, and is from the same mould as the Sniper.

Over the past year there have been several accessories introduced to the market intended to let the player replace the 12g CO_2 bulb as quickly and efficiently as possible. The WGP pump changer supplied with the Ranger differs from the other styles available to date in that it uses the push-pull of the pump handle to operate the cam action that seats the CO_2 cylinder. In a similar way to the Micro CA 2, the WGP product has a back-check valve which holds a small amount of gas in a reservoir. This gives you an extra shot or two even after the spent CO_2 bulb has been removed and is sufficient to hit the player who thinks he's caught you in the middle of a gas change. This pump changer will fit into the back bottle

▲ *WGP Ranger.*

adapter of any gun as long as it is standard thread.

Loading a 12g CO_2 bulb involves pulling the pump back about three-quarters of an inch, dropping the cylinder into the oval loading port (rear end first) and then pushing the pump forward again. When you want to change gas, point the gun down and pull the pump back which allows the spent cylinder to drop out. Substantial strength is required to eject a partially used cylinder, a heavy tug being needed.

One popular feature is that if a full cylinder is ejected with the gun held in the horizontal position, the cylinder remains in the changer with the neck angled out, and releases the gas without problems for the player who may be alongside.

Experience of the pump changer is that it is as good as anything else on the market, and substantially faster than most. The Author tested a Ranger with a 9-inch barrel although 12-inch and 14-inch are available. The 9-inch barrel together with the weight of the weapon made for good handling and excellent

accuracy. The weight of just over 3 pounds gives the weapon a good strong feel, but as most of the weight is around the grip and receiver the Ranger is a well-balanced weapon. The internals are all as standard, save for a chromed bolt mechanism. Overall the Ranger is well constructed, and great to use.

Details from: War Games Products East, PO Box 73, Holmdel, New Jersey, USA. Tel: (201) 888 1488.

THE SPLATOON

In early 1988 there was much discussion in Paintball circles regarding the legal aspects of using CO_2 as a propellant, and many people were confused as to the legality of owning CO_2 guns. Inquiries were made of the Home Office, and various replies were received

▶ *Splatoon.*

but always with the same refrain; the use of CO_2 in Paintball games was at the discretion of the Chief Constable of the particular area.

With rumour and horror stories escalating to ridiculous heights, David Pickering of Scalemead took the step of creating a new British compressed air paintball pistol: the Splatoon. This new weapon allowed site owners in England and Scotland to use clearly legal air power and thus eliminate the worry of CO_2.

This cost-efficient weapon gave site games organizers the chance to provide players with FREE AIR, for once the site has a compressor and a stock of cylinders the cost of a refill is minimal. The use of air power also eliminates the need to purchase and store large quantities of CO_2 Sparklet-type bulbs.

The Author had the opportunity to test the Splatoon and was struck by the weight of the pistol compared to American weaponry – 4.4 pounds with a stock fitted.

With a full charge in the air reservoir and loaded with a full 18-round magazine, the gun gave good results on a man-sized target from more than 30 yards away. The gun is provided with a breech porthole which allows instant verification of loading. The pump action is easy and efficient, and the .625

calibre paintball has a good flat trajectory and thus great accuracy. The gun averaged between 35 and 41 shots from each change of air, but refilling was quick and easy from the large stock cylinders. The Splatoon has adjustable velocity capability which is an extra bonus. It is quite a heavy weapon to use in pistol form, but with the shoulder-stock fitted it is easier to handle.

At the time of the test the Splatoon was one of only a handful of British-made paintball weapons and, like them, is now just another name in the history of the sport, but it could become a collectable item for the Paintball historian. The Splatoon was designed and distributed by Licensed to Thrill (UK) Ltd, 38 Roman Road, Darton, Barnsley, South Yorkshire S75 5DD.

THE BULLDOG

August 1988 saw the launch of the first all-British carbine commissioned by the Battles Games Federation and manufactured by the Colchester Air Weapon Workshop.

The Bulldog uses compressed air and thus falls in the classified air weapon section. Operating below the legal limit of 12ft/lb, it can be purchased by

▲ *Bulldog.*

anyone over the age of 17 years providing that person is a BGF member. The Bulldog is a pump-action carbine working on constant air at a power level of 8ft/lb and is fitted with a horizontal, 25-round capacity, brass-capped magazine that can be removed to allow the fitting of larger capacity gravity-fed hoppers.

The prototype Bulldog is fitted with wooden furniture, but could be converted with a skeleton stock or plastic furniture. The barrel is of steel and is 17.5 inches long, with chromed mirror finish bore and honed to .68 calibre. This gives good accuracy, and top grade ammo produces 4-inch groups at 50 yards. The Bulldog has an overall length of 33 inches and, at 8 pounds is more than three times the weight of a Phantom. The rate of fire is about 25 shots in 20 seconds when powered by a 10-inch compressed air bottle charged at 3,200psi, and the weapon fires about 120 to 150 shots per fill. The compressed air bottles used are British made and each bottle has the British Kite mark. It is vital to look for this as these are the only ones of the type that can withstand the required pressure.

Despite a successful advertising launch the Bulldog remains one of the enigmas of the British Paintball scene; most of these weapons are gathering dust in storage at one of the Action Pursuit Centres, and the Bulldog forms a strange chapter in the early history of the sport. The final chapter of these fine British weapons has yet to be written.

SANVIN SK62

When it first surfaced in May 1989, the Sanvin SK62 was unlike many of its contemporaries in that it looked like a real gun. It had a beautifully crafted

▼ *Sanvin SK62.*

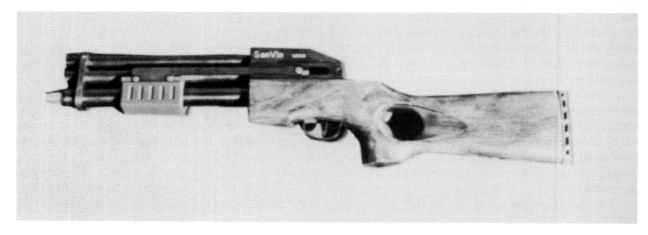

Beechwood stock, a 30cm aluminium barrel as standard and, weighing about 6½ pounds, it was not a weapon for the female player. The SK62 could be supplied with any length of barrel, from carbine to 60cm, and a magazine capable of holding 44 paintballs and a 60-shot air capacity. The standard SK62 had a 35-shot capacity with a magazine for up to 24 paintballs. Working from compressed air it is an ideal site gun as this greatly assists in keeping costs to a minimum.

At the time of manufacture the SK62, apart from the Splatoon and the Bulldog, was one of the rare precision weapons engineered in Britain from British materials. Made by San Vin Limited, Stottercliffe Road, Penistone, Sheffield, England, this paint weapon is an integral part of the early history of Paintball weaponry and, with the Bulldog, may become collectable in years to come.

SABOT CANNON

The Sabot Cannon resembles the M72A2 light anti-tank gun, but is not a real piece of army hardware; it's an actual paintball weapon.

Powered by a rechargeable CO_2 tank mounted parallel to the barrel, the Sabot is very light, being made of plastic, and despite its length is still easy to use on site.

The weapon is muzzle loaded with 10 to 15 paintballs and is gassed up with a CO_2 constant air bottle attached to the Schrader valve at the front of the gas tube. Firing is simple; press the fire button and the weapon discharges, laying down a devastating, wide-pattern 'Beehive' blast at 40 to 50 yards. A battery-operated electrically triggered firing mechanism allows remote firing as an anti-personnel mine, and paths and even the flag can be covered with the Sabot when used in 'Claymore' mode with trip-wires to booby-trap the enemy.

The cannon discharges with a loud 'whoosh' and this gives your position away. The slow reload unfortunately makes the cannon a one-shot weapon when used in fast combat, but as a support weapon or at a defence point it is easily capable of taking out a large number of the opposing team before the firer is endangered.

In the UK, Sabots were in use at the BGF Kap Young Valley site at Hookwood.

Further details from: AIR-power Sabot Cannons, 707 Wells Road, Boulder City, NV 89005, USA.

M-85 FULL AUTO

If any player has never experienced the thrill of full auto firing, one of these amazing guns is well worth seeking out. This is one weapon that is virtually impossible to own legally in the UK and this is a great pity as it has to be fired to be believed.

The Winchester large pistol primer (WLP) not only opens the bolt, ejects the fired cartridge and recocks the gun, but it also fires the 9.5mm paintball to a maximum range of 240 feet at a speed of 440fps. The rate of fire of 1,200 rounds per minute is the same as the real Mac-10 and the entire 24-round magazine is fired in 1.2 seconds. Shorter, 3–5-round, bursts are easily accomplished and are generally more effective.

Made almost entirely of hi-tech fibre filled resin impregnated with stainless steel, it is incredibly strong and totally corrosion proof. Although the M-85 has a higher muzzle velocity than any other

▼ M-85.

paintball gun, the energy of the ball or its force on impact is roughly 50–66 per cent that of the .68 calibre paintball guns. The reason for this is that the smaller 9.5mm M-85 paintball is only about one sixth of the mass of a regular .68 calibre paintball so even though it is faster it has less energy.

It is no more dangerous than any other popular paintball gun, but it is important to wear proper safety equipment when using any paintball gun. Used on the game field or on a private range, the M-85 is one of the most exciting and enjoyable guns on the market.

The M-85 is so totally realistic in its function and operation that it has been sold to motion picture and video production companies wishing safely to simulate real submachine-guns. Police, security and military customers around the world can attest to the M-85's reliability and usefulness. It loads and fires just like a real submachine-gun, allowing the trainee to learn the proper loading, firing and handling techniques in complete safety and without the added expense and inconvenience of a range or elaborate back stop. Training sessions can now be conducted almost anywhere and another advantage of the M-85 is its perfect noise level: loud enough to be effective, but not so loud as to require ear protection. Instructor and students can easily hear each other as they are unrestricted by ear plugs or bulky head sets.

For teaching the effective use of a submachine-gun or how to handle an opposing force armed with them, nothing beats actual combat experience. Laser systems and other electronic gadgets do not offer the motivation that comes with the real impact of a paintball. It is this motivation that creates the actual combat experience necessary for constructive training.

SOFTAIR 6mm PAINTBALL WEAPONRY

This area of Paintball weaponry is on the very fringe of the true sport, but as these weapons do fire paintballs it is proper that they be included. The weapons that fire the .25-inch (6mm) paintballs are the soft air replicas and most of them are made in Japan by the Tokyo Marui Co Ltd, and are sold on both sides of the Atlantic. Daisy also for a time ran a full range of soft air in this calibre, but the 'toy gun' laws of the States knocked the bottom out of the market for this type of air weaponry, although there is a growing market with replica weapon collectors in the UK.

For a short time Battle Orders Ltd in the UK and The Command Post in the USA marketed the 6mm paintballs in this micro calibre. They were sold in tubs of 50 in red or blue, but a major problem with the

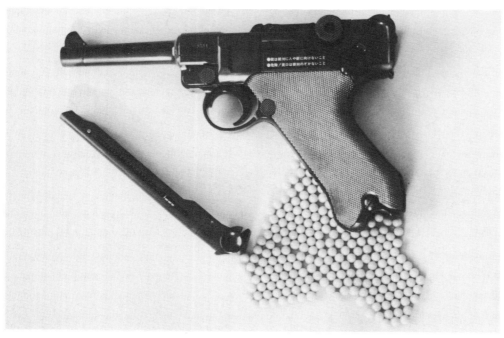

◄ *Luger P.08.*

▲ SA 80.

micro-sized ammo was that it was excellent for repro soft air weaponry, made to fire 6mm nylon/plastic balls, but when a breakage occurred, the fill of the paint completely blocked the internals of the weapon.

The Author has yet to come across any user who has a good word for 6mm Paintball ammo.

The soft air weapons that fire 6mm are well worth a look. The H&K MP5 from Daisy, and the Luger P.08 from Command Post both look as real as they feel.

The H&K MP5 has slide pump cocking action, and fires 12 6mm balls from a cartridge clip. At short range in the back garden the low muzzle velocities of both these soft air weapons make them perfect for plinking. The Luger has a 15-shot magazine, and for its size and low spring power is extremely accurate.

For a full-sized replica of the British Army SA80 with Susat-type sight and full working action in 6mm, made in metal and ABS, requiring no licence to own and fire (soft air power .04 joules) and sold fully assembled together with a 30-round magazine, contact Graham Barton, Battle Orders Ltd, 71a Eastbourne Road, Lower Willingdon, Eastbourne, East Sussex, BN20 9NR. Tel: 03212 5182.

LS55 LASERSIGHT

The compact LS55 adds an accurate point and shoot capability to paintball weapons. Used exactly as in military, police and special forces world-wide, simply pick out the target with an intense dot of visible laser light and open fire. With the dot on target you can be sure of getting your paintball on target every time. The continuous beam or battery-saving pulse mode gives an easy to see flashing dot and by simplifying and speeding the aim, the LS55 makes every shot count. It is faster than conventional optical sighting methods and enhances your marksmanship. In the smoke given off by pyros or early morning mist, the beam as well as the dot can be seen, and in the deceptive low light conditions experienced at dusk or dawn, in the shaded areas of a wood or an indoors site the LS55 offers instantaneous target acquisition.

Field testing proves that the LS55 gains psychological dominance over your opponents for as soon as the enemy sees the red dot appear on them, the target is convinced that the paintball will instantly follow. The result is that return fire is wild as the target only wants to shake off the dot. In some cases the dot itself create a degree of panic and is an established combat deterrent.

As a light-emitting device, the LS55 is intended for use in low light conditions or where there is no

▲ *LS 55 Lasersight.*

light. In bright daylight the dot is hardly visible, so the LS55 can be co-located with other sights to enhance the capability of your weapon system.

Specifications:

Size: 176mm (7 inches) long; 25mm (1 inch) barrel diameter.

Switching: 175mm (6⅞ inches) long, cable & pressure switch,

Switch is fitted with adhesive tape to mount to the most convenient part of the weapon for thumb or finger activation by right or left hand. The pulse mode selector switch is located within the LS55 housing.

Alignment: less than 25mm spot at 20 metres (1 inch at 22 yards). Clickscrew adjustment 6mm at 45 metres (¼ inch at 50 yards).

Output Beam: Wavelength typically 670mm (blood red) Class III limit (not greater than 5mW throughout). Output aperture approximately 6mm (¼ inch). Beam divergence 0.5m Rad.

Battery life: 3 × AAA Alkaline batteries (3 × LOR3) yield a battery life of up to 9 hours in continuous use (16 hours in pulse mode).

Mounting: LS55 is designed to fit any pair of standard 1-inch scope rings mounted on a weapon. Being so compact, it can be mounted below the barrel on many weapons. Slightly offset, it can be co-located with other sights as required. When high profile 1-inch scope rings are selected, iron sights are not obstructed.

The LS55 Lasersight is designed, developed and manufactured by Imatronic, a world leader in opto-electronics. Full details from: Imatronic Limited, Kingfisher Court, Hambridge Road, Newbury, Berkshire RG14 5SJ. In USA: Imatronic Incorporated, PO Box 520, 1275 Paramount Parkway, Batavia, Illinois 60510, USA.

FOCAL POINT SIGHTS

With the purchase of a single-point sight in June 1981 the Author's snap shooting improved overnight. An improved sight, the Cyclops, was simpler and uncomplicated. This operates on the reflex principle, gathering and concentrating natural light through a reticle light-box positioned on top of the sight. Light is directed through the reticle on to a mirror and back to the shooter's eye. The secret of the sight is the unique, gold-coloured mirror that not only reflects the reticle image but allows the shooter to look through the mirror at the target. No batteries are required because daylight illuminates the reticle to a bright pink fluorescent colour and makes sighting very easy. For mounting the Cyclops on the weapon the only tool required was a 2p coin. Because of production problems, this sight was not on sale for very long and the ones still in circulation are rapidly becoming much sought-after collectables.

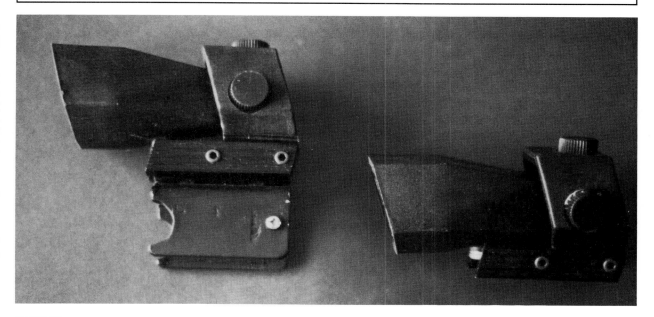

▲ Focal point sights.

This was the situation until 1986 when a new sight made by Focal Point Armoury Limited appeared. This new sight is a lightweight (109g) including a non-creep mount. It comes with screwdriver and Allen key for fitting.

With the Focal Point Gold fitted to a rifle, the weapon has a rather futuristic appearance and can produce some rather startled looks on site. The test involved placing empty cans at 20 yards' range and then at 5-yard intervals up to 30 yards. Firing was so easy that adjustments were not necessary; from the first shot the cans went down.

The Focal Point Gold is very fast aiming; no bulb or batteries are required and the light source is guaranteed for ten years. Even spray or rain on the lens does not decrease its effectiveness because, unlike a telescopic sight which requires a clear lens to see the target, the player does not view the target through the Focal Point because the aiming point is directed back into the eye. The speed a little practise brings makes the sight one of the fastest currently on a non-military weapon.

The Focal Point Gold is a civilian version of a combat-proven sighting system. The image that you see is the standard red dot image, the dot produced by a Beta lamp, a red dye that is light-gathering, mounted on an acrylic stick which is illuminated at night by Beta lights. This presents the shooter's master eye with a red dot which is mentally superimposed over the target. This is far better than the red dot produced by some laser sighting systems as only the shooter sees the red dot image.

There is also no fear of laser beams bouncing back and revealing the location of the shooter. The system hits objects of varying sizes over all the distances you could expect an air weapon to perform. As the red dot has no maximum range the range of the sight is only limited by the flat trajectory of your ammunition. The sight is not designed to replace the telescopic sight for long-distance accurate shooting, but is intended more as a fast game sight.

Following the Focal Point Gold came the Focal Point Splat. As most Paintball sites operate only in daylight hours the new Splat sight does not employ the Beta light module but an enlarged red dot. This makes the sight even faster to use, especially in close-combat in dense vegetation.

Focal Point Armoury has a history of supplying the military market with hi-tech systems, and in the Paintball sector their experts have been swift to use British technology and expertise. The economic climate in the UK at present is not so accommodating, and Focal Point do not retail the sight in the UK.

For full details of this sight in the USA contact: Night Owl Action Enterprises Incorporated, 14915 Aurora Avenue, North Seattle, WA 98133. Tel: (206) 367 4997.

MODEL 800 POINT SIGHT

The Model 800 Point Sight is made by Daisy Manufacturing Company of the United States. Experience of many sites in the UK and Europe has shown this sight to be one of the most popular accessory optics to be fitted to paintball guns. Some of the major features are:

1 Fully adjustable for windage and elevation.
2 Packed with extra reticles.
3 Mounts easily to any gun with standard ⅜ dovetail mount.
4 Lightweight carbon graphite material.
5 Permits both eyes open firing.

Critical Specifications:
1 The Point Sight is a reflecting translucent glass mirror lens with a rear image point 1:1 ratio.
2 Can be used on both rifles and pistols (pistols require simple adaptors).
3 Suitable for both beginners and experienced shooters — just sight in reticle pattern on target and fire.
4 No batteries needed.

General Specifications:
1 Eye relief non-critical, parallax free.
2 Number of lenses: single.
3 Length: 4.46 inches (11.43cm).
4 Weight: 2oz.

This super sight is very easy to fit and use and once zeroed, you superimpose a small orange image over your target where the paintball is to hit, and squeeze the trigger. A range of alternative reticles are supplied with the sight.

For details contact: Daisy Manufacturing Company, Box 220, Rogers, AR 72757 0220 USA.

INTER-AIMS Mk 5 SIGHT

Made for Malmos, Sweden, by Inter-Aims, the Mk 5 sight is a piece of quality equipment designed by Swedish craftsmen and it can really make the average shot into a formidable marksman.

Originally intended for the hunting market, this sight has come into its own in the Paintball market. As the sport grows many more players seem willing to invest money in their weapons systems and the Inter Aims sight is worthy of serious consideration.

The Mk 5 is mounted on standard 1-inch ring mounts and standard mount bases. On rifles where

there is a long distance between the bases a tube extension is provided which is screwed into the front part of the sight to increase its overall length. Adjustment for windage and elevation is provided by coin slot adjustment screws which have protective covers. If the sight was fitted to a centre-fire rifle, rather than a paintball weapon, turning the adjustment screw by one mark would move the point of impact about a quarter of an inch at 110 yards. The brightness and intensity of the red dot is adjustable by means of a potentiometer knob which also serves as an on-off switch. Proper use of this facility involves adjusting it to as low an intensity as your eye will register.

Avoid having the dot too bright, especially during low light conditions. For shooting in bright sunshine and towards a white background, the intensity of the red dot can be increased by means of a bi-packed polarised filter. The sight comes equipped with two mercury batteries, which will last from 50 to 10,000 hours depending on the intensity used for the red dot.

A little time is needed to zero this sight for Paintball use because it was designed for greater distances and flatter trajectories, but once set up the sight performs very well.

For full details in the UK contact the UK Agent on Tel: 0424 753588.

SHARPSHOOTER GUN SIGHT

Airgun Designs, manufacturers of the PMI Face Shield and Micro-CA, have now come up with a new sight called 'The Sharpshooter'; an innovative ⅜-inch dove-tail groove open sight and designed specifically for Paintball weaponry. Although firing in Paintball games is instinctive, there are times when one needs the tracking of the first shot to know where to place the second just as there are occasions when a carefully placed shot is required. This is where the Sharpshooter comes in to its own. The sight comes fully assembled in its box, ready for installation. If you have a gun provided with a sight rail, you simply loosen off the bolts on the side of the sight, slide the sight on to the rail, and retighten the bolts.

If your gun does not have a sight rail, your local Paintball accessories or gun shop should have a small length that can be bolted or glued to the barrel of your gun.

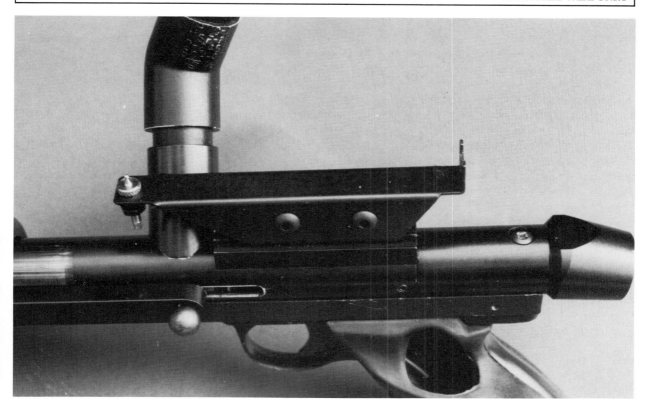

▲ Sharpshooter.

While testing the sight, and matching it to various Paintball guns, one concern was that guns with thin mounting rails or with dove-tail mounting slots machined into their barrels/receivers, such as the SMG-60, might not be able to accept the Sharpshooter due to its thick steel sides. Careful flat draw filing of the lower edges of the clamping corners to obtain sharper, but still blunt edges will allow solid clamping of the sight. The brass sight pin at the front of the unit is held in place by two nuts. The largest of these, when loosened, will allow the pin to slide left or right so that you can adjust for windage. The smaller nut, when loosened, will allow the sight pin to be screwed up or down to adjust for elevation. Do not over-tighten these nuts or the brass parts will suffer damage.

The Sharpshooter sight plane is lower than many of the accessory sights tested and one small fault is that the red paint on the foresight bead rubbed off after a little use. The unguarded construction of the front pin risks early damage from use on site.

The rear butterfly on the sight has a step arrangement to allow targeting at three distances: short, medium and long range. By aligning the front-sight ball with the bottom of the rear butterfly, you are set for a short-range shot with minimum ball drop to the target. The same is true for a mid-range shot from the middle step, and a long-range shot from the top of the rear sight. Airgun Designs recommend that you adjust the sight at the mid-range step for the distance you feel to be the average distance for which you shoot. Once at this setting, move physically closer to your target until the bottom sight starts shooting into the bull.

Make a mental note of the distance and repeat with long-range shots. Finally, adjust windage by sliding the pin from side to side. In some cases, you may want to sight your Sharpshooter at a distance beyond its scope of adjustment. This is most likely to happen with the longer shots that cause the ball to drop out of range before striking the target. If this is the case, carefully bend the rear butterfly up, and continue the sighting-in procedure.

For further information contact: Airgun Designs, 301 Industrial Lane, Wheeling, IL 60090, USA.

▲ *Smoke pyro.*

PYROTECHNICS

In the early days of UK Paintball the use of pyros on site was an unknown quantity because the only items in this specialized field were ex-military and consequently were not designed for sporting use. The charge in the thunder flashes was enough to literally make the hair stand on end. For the novice a breakdown of the basics would be most helpful, and the Oxford Dictionary lists pyrotechnic as a firework. There are three categories of Paintball pyros:

1 'Flash/Bang' hand-thrown thunder flash or fuzed black powder mine.
2 'Bang/Splat' paint grenade or anti-personnel mine.
3 'Smoke'.

Although other types exist, these basic three are the most commonly encountered on the Paintball site.

SMOKE

The smoke 'bomb' is the most used Paintball pyro and is a tactical weapon which can have great impact on the game. Most have a protective sleeve which is easily removable and a striker which is drawn over the friction end to ignite the bomb. Some pyros have a secondary burn which is an advantage because often the smoke on this type will fail if thrown instantly.

As always, experience of brands will soon determine which is best. On test the white smoke was most widely used and gave the longer burn time,

▶ *Ground-burst.*

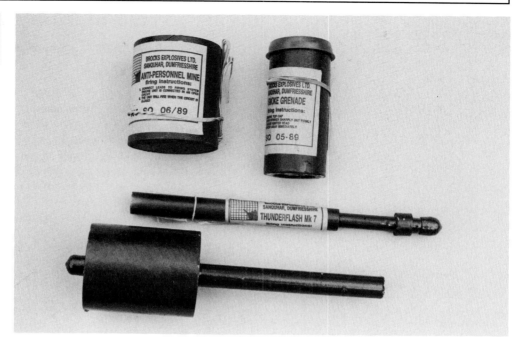

▶ *Paint mine, smoke-grenade, thunderflash and paint-grenade.*

but does not lend itself to photographic uses as well as others.

PAINT MINES AND GRENADES

The principal weapons in this category are the hand-thrown paint grenade and the battery-detonated anti-personnel mine. The hand-thrown paint grenade resembles the German stick grenade of the Second World War and is relatively straightforward to use: remove the top cap, draw the striker sharply across the igniter head and then throw away immediately. The anti-personnel mine is virtually the same weapon, but is detonated by a small battery detonator pack, or a PP3 battery. The advantage of these pyros is that it is easy to mine the Flag and have a bomber concealed in the undergrowth to splat any enemy in the danger zone.

Thunder Flash This pyro is familiar to many players and most ex-army and service personnel will have used the Thunder Flash Mk 8. This little device was used where a loud report and bright flash were required, such as in realistic grenade training. The Author would like to take this opportunity strongly to condemn the use of any type or brand of military thunder flash on a Paintball site. The 12g explosive content is just too powerful for non-military use. The special Paintball 'thunder flashes' should be used on

site because the small explosive content is quite loud enough. If the worst does happen and a player falls to an ignited thunder flash Paintball charge, the only injury will be to his pride.

Of all the pyros available there is still a concern over untrained personnel throwing any type of thunder flash. With all sites striving to keep a high safety record, the use of this type of item in untrained hands is still a worry. When used by trained marshals during a game they can, however, really add to the excitement. This is not only the safest way to use this type of weaponry, but the marshals can also use them more effectively with the right number at the right time. Using a little imagination and presetting the site with charges, a very small area of woodland can become an explosive experience for even the most hardened Paintball veteran.

The use of remote-controlled detonation quickly makes the player wary and careful of movements on site. For the regular player, however, the use of smoke should be considered carefully as constant exposure to certain smokes can cause health problems because of toxic and irritant chemicals emitted as the smoke-genade burns.

The pyros made by Brocks Explosives Ltd are among the very best and are some of the very few which have been passed as safe for use in the USA. If you are playing constantly, week in, week out, and

▲ *Paint-grenade.*   ▼ *Playmore mine.*

value your lungs and don't want to have health problems caused by excessive exposure to smoke, make sure the pyros you use are non-toxic and non-irritant. Pyros in this section were supplied by: Brocks Explosives Ltd, Sanquhar, Dumfries, Scotland DG4 6JP.

Storage of pyrotechnics The laws governing the use and storage of pyrotechnics with particular reference to Paintball sites were explained by A. Green, at that time commercial sales engineer of Brocks Explosives Ltd. Under the Explosives Act 1875 (amended 1923) and legislation introduced since 1941, sites can store explosives under local authority licence. The matter has been discussed with the Health and Safety Executive who are responsible for matters concerning explosives within the UK, and provided the quantity is less than 1,800kg (net explosive content), a competent local authority officer such as the Standards Officer or local Fire Authority Chief can authorize the licence.

All sites using pyrotechnics in any quantity should hold a Stores Licence to allow the storage of pyrotechnics, or, as a minimum, hold a Registered Premises Certificate. The latter is again under the province of local authorities and allows the storage of between 45kg and 90kg nett explosive content.

A Fit Person's Certificate must be obtained from the local police authority before applying for either type of licence. The Explosives Act is very complex, and to stay on the right side of the law it is advisable to study it in close detail with regard to the site and its requirements.

PAINT MINE AND PAINT GRENADES

On a special pyrotechnic course these items were tested in field conditions. The mine is of the anti-personnel paint type and is detonated by battery or detonator pack. Triggered at 15 feet the mine gives good coverage — 5-metre spread of yellow paint. The test personnel shown in the photograph demonstrate the effectiveness of this pyro. Although the explosion from the charge is loud, the power of this mine is quite safe and in no way jeopardizes safety standards.

Hand (paint) grenade This is one pyro that does look like the real thing. Made of expanded polystyrene, this hand-thrown grenade is great to

▶ *Typical mine detonation system.*

use. The firing instructions are: remove the dummy plastic top handle and pin, which come off in one piece. Draw the striker sharply across the igniter head and throw the grenade immediately. The structure of this pyro on explosion completely breaks up and after test only one very small fragment of the casing could be found. It was so light that it would not register on the scales and this is a major bonus for the safety record for this item.

The grenade consists of an expanded polystyrene outer body with a cardboard top cap on which is painted the phosphorus striking composition. The centrally located burster/sound unit consists of a cardboard tube with 0.5g of Flash Composition and a Bickford fuzed delay, similar to a thunder flash. The grenade is also filled with a dye in a sealed polythene bag. The dye is manufactured in the USA as a Bentone EW Rheological additive (Hectorite) and is used extensively in toiletry and cosmetic applications. It is approved under FDA Regulations 21 (F 175.105, 16.170 and 176.180).

The dye anti-personnel mine This consists of an expanded polystyrene outer body, 150mm × 75mm diameter, with a centrally located burster unit comprised of a cardboard tube containing approximately 4g of flash powder, a 50/50 mixture of Aluminium dark powder and Potassium Perchlorate. Initiation is by way of an electrically fired fuze, the mine being filled with dye contained in a sealed polythene bag. For full details contact: Pyro Supplies UK. Tel: 0424 753588.

NON-PYROTECHNIC MINES AND GRENADES

The 'Playmore-Mine' is ideal for sites that run into problems with local councils or zone boards. With no explosive used in this weapon, it would be difficult to find a more acceptable alternative pyrotechnic.

The Playmore-Mine comes complete with everything you need to use except the paint. Simply fill the syringe-type filler with paint, remove the bottom of the mine and fill the tube through a special pressure valve and replace the bottom. When ready to use remove the pin, set the trip-wire and wait for an opponent to spring the trap. Upon release the mine sprays a large plume of paint.

Squad buster grenade This is another great addition to the non-pyro grenade market, and it really does live up to its name. It gives the capability to splat as many players as can be found in a 25-foot radius. There is no immunity from this grenade as it touches almost everything. The grenade uses a twin pressurized bladder system full of washable blue paint. Just pull the pin and toss this grenade in the general direction of the opposing team. If one or more players are grouped close together, this will spin and flip enough to spray all of them.

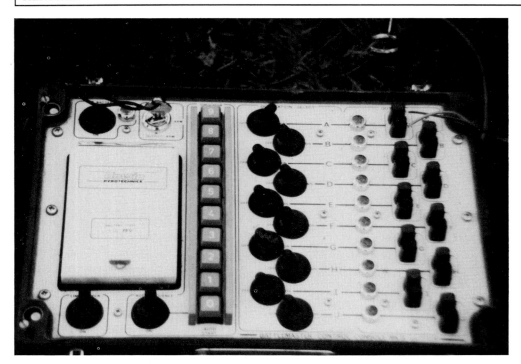

◄ *Pyro control console.*

THE SPI PAINT-MINE

Simulated Pursuit Industries of Florida have developed this paint-mine for specific use on the Paintball site. The mine works with one or two pints of paint and 100psi of air pressure. To fill the mine unscrew the central detonator (tool provided) and measure out the paint. Screw the detonator back in position and fix the safety-pin in place. Now add air which can be done with a cycle pump, although it is wise to have a reliable pressure gauge to check the pressure.

On test the mine was fired with pressures as low as 50psi with good results as the paint spread was 25 feet. At 100psi the measured spread reached 50 feet so it is possible to manipulate the pressure and paint fill to get the effect you require. Recharging the mine takes less than five minutes, considerably less with practice. The mine is easy to place and fire and the best results occur when the mine is set into the ground with the trip-plate barely visible. This gives the mine stability, and allows the deployment of trip-wires. These when triggered allow the central paint distributor to push up and force the strike plate to the side.

For full information contact: Simulated Pursuit Industries, 4964 Kirk Road, Lake Worth, Florida 33461, USA.

TRAILBLAZER PAINT-MINE

The Trailblazer from GMRJ Enterprises is lightweight, re-usable and easy to clean. Not only can you re-use it with biodegradable paint, but you can also recharge the mine with a portable air tank, regulated CO_2, or a tyre pump. Once triggered, the mine explodes over 5 seconds, covering an arc of 140 degrees in a 15-foot radius over 300 square feet.

For more details contact: GMRJ Enterprises, 2022–20th Avenue North, Lethbridge, Alberta, Canada.

BOUNCING BERTHA PAINT-GRENADE

This grenade is of the same design as the original 'Bouncing Betty', but is twice the size. Use is simplicity itself: pull the pin, take the cap off and throw it. On impact it sprays paint in all directions. The Bertha grenade is not an explosive or splash-type balloon as each tube is pressurized and sprays orange, biodegradable, water-soluble paint over 30 feet.

For further information contact: Pro Star Labs, RMT Sports, PO Box 1281, Littleton, Colorado 80160, USA.

Safety First

In many publications and brochures issued by Paintball organisers it is alarming to see group pictures of players posing with weapons pointed at one another's heads. After years of firearms training the Author has never used this type of photograph. Weapon safety should be top priority on all sites and even displaying this type of photograph is a step in the wrong direction. Media reporters often try to get this pose but it will only be used in coverage that is not to the good of the sport and should be avoided. Also avoid using phrases such as 'kills made', instead use 'hits' because some journalists will try to report the sports as something quite different.

On most sites the goggles supplied will have the British Standard Kite Mark and the numbers BS4110. There will also be a couple of extra letters which indicate the level of testing to which the lens has been subjected. There is also an American equivalent which will be shown on all goggles imported from the USA. In the UK the testing of a lens is conducted by using a 6.5mm steel ball to test the impact resistance of the lenses at various speeds:
BS4100XA: 12mps/27mph equivalent to low protection from small flying objects.
BS4110YA: 45mps/10mph, equivalent to medium protection from small flying objects.
BS5110ZA: 70mps/15mph, equivalent to good pro-

▶ Fem-Guard.

tection from small flying objects.

(mps = metres per second; mph = miles per hour). The 'A' indicates that the lens has passed an abrasion test in BS4110.

Some goggles made by Uvex UK Limited have the letter '/Z' at the end of the BS number, indicating a high impact tested goggle. Never ever wear a goggle with '/I' which indicates a low impact type and is not intended for Paintball games.

Most regular players buy their own safety gear. For newcomers considering taking up the sport it is in your own interests to obtain and use your own equipment on which you can rely, and which you know suits you as an individual. Everyone has his own preference for protection on site, but over and above that preference it is worth taking the trouble to ensure that the equipment selected is the very best available.

It is wise to take the trouble to visit suppliers and try the products first hand to make sure they fit your requirements. Alternatively, if you see a player on site with a good item of kit it may be possible to try it to make sure that it does meet the claims of the glossy advertisements.

One valuable item of safety head wear is the 'Carbon Copy' Paintball helmet. This weighs only 7oz (200gm) but gives good protection to the face and ears. The Author has a personal interest in this item of kit as he was once shot while playing at close range early in his Paintball career. A stray shot to the jaw caused a bruise that lasted a week. It seemed advisable to prevent the same thing happening again and the helmet was ordered from Tom Campagna in America. When it arrived it was given an immediate and realistic field test. Using an NGS Savage at 12 feet, then 9 feet, and finally 6 feet — 'point-blank' — no injury was sustained other than three tiny cuts to the forehead by fragments of the gelatin outers of the paintballs breaking up on the edge of the goggles. The fact that ten head shots were taken and easily deflected at close range proves that this item of equipment is very sturdy despite its light weight. The Carbon Copy Helmet can be purchased from Carbon Copy, 31139 W. Via Colinas, Suite 203, Westlake Village, CA 91362, USA. As with all items of safety kit it is best to try before you buy and discover your personal preferences.

To date the safety record of the sport has been very good, and it is essential that at every initial briefing players are made aware of the paramount importance of eye protection. Replacement goggles should also be carried by all marshals to that an instant changeover can be effected if the need arises.

There are two other items that come under the heading of safety wear: both are widely used in America but not much as yet in the UK. The first is for female players and is called the 'Fem-Guard' and is a protective bra. The ventilated Urethane cups are worn over the regular bra and underneath other clothing. They are lightweight and washable, and give excellent discreet protection.

The second item is for male players and is a groin cup with supporter similar to that worn in cricket. These items can be purchased from I & I Sports in Los Angeles Tel: (313) 732 7212.

There is nothing cowardly about wearing protective equipment: you would not expect a soldier to enter battle without his helmet or a pro-football player in a game without his safety equipment. The Paintballer is free to choose what protection he or she wants to wear. Players with good protection will not feel their injuries and consequently will not put other potential players off.

Now, in the nineties, there are many manufacturers producing camo 'protective' clothing, but for kit with style certain items take some beating. Richard Hockley played his first game of Paintball in 1987 and soon saw the need for a redesign of the web gear, belt and pouches, camo suit and neck protecter. He designed a suit to meet his needs and after realizing that there was no product like it, he started up in business with Hock Bo Arms.

Now the company makes virtually everything on the Paintball clothing market, including custom gear, accommodating paint tubes, grenades, bulk loaders and any specialized work to fit the players' needs. When interviewed he said: 'I started the company with the intention of making the best camo clothing that anyone could afford. For what you get the prices are low. A lot of time is put into every garment and I don't cut costs by using poor quality material. A lot of thread and time goes into every suit and vest.' The truth behind this is revealed in the latest design: the new Fall and Winter insulated camo jump-suit with extra padding.

An extra touch is that the upper tube pouch is strategically placed to protect the chest area. Each suit has a pouch on the upper thigh to hold four CO_2 bulbs and is Velcro fastened. These battle suits are

► *JT Body armour.*

lightly padded on the upper body, front and back, with a collar that can be snapped as a neck protecter during the game. Each suit has a 22-inch front zipper for easy access, and is designed for the novice and pro-player alike. Two lower chest pouches hold 12 paint tubes and two upper chest pouches hold eight CO_2 bulbs. Again, they are lightly padded both front and back and a special lightweight summer net/battle vest is also available.

Custom-made orders can be requested to fit individual need and style and the player can take the basic suit and add pouches for paint tubes, grenades, spare parts and CO_2 bulbs, with extra padding on the knees and elbows as required. The suit is available in: woodland, marsh, desert, black, tree bark, tiger stripe, and Fall and Winter designs, and full details come from Richard Hockley, HockBo Arms, 1833 Harmony Drive, Fort Collins, CO 80525, USA.

◄ *The Author's wife demonstrating good face and hands protection.*

Camouflage

Camo gear is very difficult to photograph successfully, its very purpose being to blend in with the surroundings. Many readers of this book may well be new to the Paintball scene, but an important lesson to learn early on is the value of camouflage.

As Paintball increases in popularity, so too increases the sophistication of players and the equipment they use and wear. Gone are the days when camo was the first bit of ex-Government clothing available. Today's Paintball enthusiast uses every development possible to help him/her in the sport and effective camo is guaranteed to get you closer to your quarry.

Selection of the right type of camouflage clothing for any given area is more than choosing 'woodland' for woodland areas. In certain tests at 50 metres or over, woodland camouflage in a woodland setting stands out as an unnatural dark blob, whereas the black, white and grey of ASAT camo blends in well because the light and dark patches resemble tree limbs. Using white and grey grease paint renders the player virtually undetectable.

ASAT (All Season All Terrain) is a completely new concept in camouflage clothing and is the result of eight years of patient, exhaustive research. What began as a curiosity turned into a long search for a 'single' camouflage pattern which would work successfully during each of the four seasons in all sub-arctic environments of North America and other parts of the world.

Initially this seemed to be an impossible task since research findings indicated two limiting factors. The first was that all traditional military and civilian camouflages were ineffective even in their most suitable environments beyond a distance of 12 yards. After that point, the individual parts of the camo pattern tend to merge together and the person became a dark patch that actually stood out and called attention to its position in the environment. The condition was aggravated if the person were on a ridge line or silhouetted against the sky.

The second problem, assuming that these traditional patterns were effective in a limited way, was the cost factor. The dedicated camo user would have to purchase, and eventually replace at least two and often four different sets of camo in order to meet his needs. This would be cost-prohibitive for peacetime military budgets where requirements were for both woods-related and desert-related clothing.

The solution to these problems was ASAT camouflage. With large blotches of colour, high tonal contrast between the three colours in the pattern, and the pattern shape which complements more than 90 per cent of the shapes found in nature, ASAT is truly a camouflage for all seasons and all terrain.

There are always critics of any camo pattern, and I expect there will be critics of ASAT. However, the extensive testing of prototype ASAT garments in the Canadian forests of the east to the high country of the Rocky Mountains in the west, has proven conclusively that ASAT will perform in a highly superior manner in any location at any time of the year.

Humans see everything subjectively, interpreting what is seen not only on the basis of what is there, but also based upon emotional conditions, mental state, prior experience and other factors. What one person sees can be interpreted and described in a totally different style by another. But the camera sees totally objectively and the photographs that result from the camera's work are factual representations of what existed in that place and at that time.

◄ *Day time woodland camouflage — note good hands cover.*

To prove the value of ASAT yourself, perform the following test: take your favourite military or commercial camo pattern suit into the terrain and environment you often visit. Take a suit of ASAT as well. Then you, and if possible a friend, take turns wearing and viewing both suits from various positions for each pattern. If you have a camera load it with colour film and take several photographs of each type of camo suit under the same conditions. For example with a tree trunk directly behind, in a tree stand or similarly elevated position or silhouetted against the sky. Take these shots at distances of 10, 20, 30 and 40 or more yards. When you receive the finished prints you will have the factual proof that ASAT really works.

Camouflaging the face

Paintball sites usually have a variety of facial camo available, ranging from the 'Black and White Minstrel' to Vietnam. Some players, particularly those with a forces background, do get it right, but many beginners seem to work on the principle of smearing on as much camo cream as possible and hoping for the best. A non-camouflaged face is particularly dangerous during night games, because the skin will reflect sufficient light to give your position away. Even on a very dark night a sudden flash from a thunder flash or a para flare will light up the face as if hit by a torch beam. It was once thought that smearing mud on the face was a good way to conceal it at night. However,

▶ *American player with apex weaponry — again good camo.*

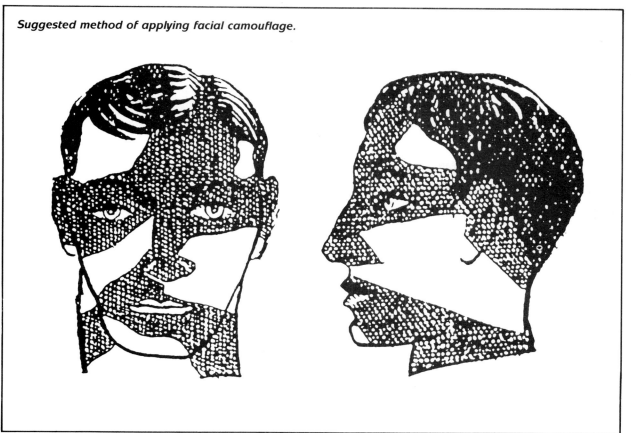

Suggested method of applying facial camouflage.

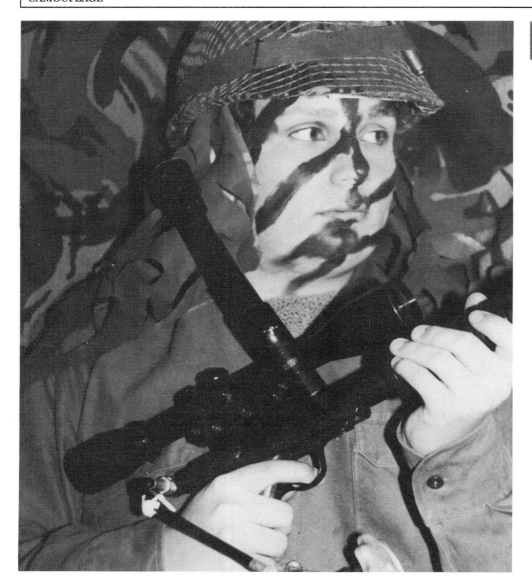

◀ *Posed night camo sniper — poor hands.*

this is only to be recommended in the last resort for mud dries to a very light colour and after only ten minutes it can make your face stand out more clearly than if you had used nothing at all. In desperation the keen player can use cow dung which does not dry out to a light colour, but has obvious disadvantages.

It is not advisable to use 'Spandoflage' or any other type of net over the face at night because although the net does not so interfere with vision as to be a nuisance in daylight, it certainly does at night. In the dark the eyes must not be hindered in the slightest degree in distinguishing between slight differences of tone. Any net sufficiently thick to be

useful as camouflage will be too thick for the eyes.

When applying camo cream the first rule is that good results do not follow from simply smearing camo cream all over the face. The requirement is for a pattern with sharp outlines. The parts of the face to be painted should be completely covered leaving no thin places: the parts of the face left bare should have no smears of paint on them.

Concealing pattern

The following is a description of the concealing pattern taught to the Author while in the Falklands.
1 The eyes are concealed by a 'V'-shaped line carried

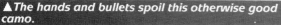
▲ The hands and bullets spoil this otherwise good camo.

▲ Good overall camo is let down by poor hands and neck.

back to the ears. The whole eyelid and the part between the eyes and nose must be painted or the eyes really stand out. The upper lid must not be forgotten for every time you blink it resembles the flashing of a small light.

2 The nose must be well painted out.

3 The pattern should be different for each side of the face to destroy tell-tale symmetry. The ideal is to alter the general shape so much that the enemy will not think that any bright object is a human face.

4 Remember that it is easier to work on your colleague's face, and vice versa, than trying to apply camo yourself.

Remember that camouflage is difficult to get off, especially if you only have cold stream or lake water to work with. Once you've got the hang of face camouflage you should be completely invisible in daylight at 50 metres, and at night the enemy should have to step on you before they realize you are there.

While on the subject of night games one further point is that it is fine to cover the face in camo cream, but a skilful application is wasted if the hands stand out. Hands are a danger point for two reasons. First due to their lightness of tone, and secondly because they are the part of the body which is moved by the untrained player advancing across rough country. It is still a mistake to darken the hands all over for the same reason that it is not advisable to overdo facial camo. To break up the even surface paint stripes down the fingers and over the wrists as this will help to make them less conspicuous.

Experience shows that fingerless gloves are also a good way of stopping the hand reflecting the light. If you are using a constant air weapon with a large tank system, it is also wise to mask out the shiny brass fittings as these can be a clear give-away under certain light conditions on night games. Also avoid standing next to a gap in a hedge or wall as even at night it is amazing how clearly the silhouette stands out. Most newcomers to night games make the mistake of dressing all in black and thinking that they are invisible. However, the true key to remaining undetected is movement. Imagine the movements of a cat when stalking: it moves softly and slowly when

◄ *The Author demonstrates good dusk camo while in the safe zone.*

it has to move, but when there is a chance of detection it remains frozen. New players will need to practise this because standing still is not a natural state for most people. An example is to watch the first-time player when being briefed. If his feet are still he will certainly be moving his head or neck, scratching an ear or fidgeting in some way with his hands or arms. It is these useless fidgeting movements that you must avoid.

The best way to avoid being seen is to find a tree or bush to hide behind. Other than that, drab green clothing is better than black-based camo, and this tip is guaranteed by training undertaken by the Author with a concealment expert. If using a night scope of any sort remember that the lens often glints in the dark and the reflection can give away your position. It is often best to keep the lens cap on until you are ready to fire.

Before attempting to get close to the enemy team, take the precaution of checking all your camouflage, personal clothing and weapon. Make sure that your equipment will not rattle or snag and remember that a full ammo hopper or tube will make

◀ *The HockBo Arms suit.*

▼ *Night camo for special training exercise.*

◄ *Night camo ruined by the hands.*

less noise than a part-filled hopper as the balls will not move about. It is wise to go easy with camo tape on your weapon, the enthusiastic novice can often impair the efficiency of the weapon by overdoing it. Check before playing the game that your clothing is 'soft', flexible and comfortable as baggy gear is easily snagged by undergrowth and brambles. Once you are satisfied that you are as well concealed as possible you have to crawl to the most effective position from which to get a shot and this involves a calculated risk. It is vital to weigh up the advantage to be gained against the chance of attracting the attention of the enemy team and drawing their fire.

When really close to the enemy team, crawling on hands and knees is best carried out thus:
(A) Lay your Paintball weapon on the ground. Use your right hand to feel for a clear place for your right knee.
(B) Keeping your hand in place, bring your knee forward until it touches the hand. Repeat the process with your left hand and knee.
(C) As you progress, move your weapon by feeling for and clearing a place, then lifting the weapon slowly and carefully into position.

Remember to make all movements in slow motion, and one of the most difficult things to remember is that when not moving it is vital to be absolutely motionless. The only way to learn this lesson is to watch other players in a game and then watch a cat waiting at a mousehole. Only then is the difference between human and animal fieldcraft obvious.

Until you have learned to imitate the cat, you will fidget. You will scrach at a fly behind your ear, you will finger your gun, you will turn your head from side to side unnecessarily, you will adjust your equipment as if about to be photographed. Then the position you have got into is not as comfortable as

▲ *Day camo for a special exercise.*

▲ *Good overall camo, note hands and faces.*

you first thought, and a new one is sought and then if you move your foot a bit to the right you will get an even better view. These are all fatal mistakes and any one may cost you the game.

Provided you have the bare minimum of natural cover you are safe as long as you remain still, but even the movement of your head from side to side is enough to give your position away. You should concentrate on becoming perfect at remaining motionless. Remember too that this 'freezing-up' is quite different from standing to attention: there should be nothing strained about it. You should waste no energy moving, partly because movement gives you away to the opposing team, and partly because with your body in complete inactivity all the energy is concentrated upon thought, sight and hearing.

From photographing many hundreds of games the Author has noticed that a sure test of a player's training is if he stops still or fidgets when being briefed. A well-trained player does not stand stiffly nor does he move about when a game is being explained to him. He gives the impression of bodily repose while his mind is active. This is very important to learn because any part of you not being used at a given moment should be resting. The result is that the strain is not so great when the action begins. The art of remaining motionless is important so as not to reveal your position and also to allow concentration and rest at the same time.

Many players use ex-army helmets, as advertised in most of the Paintball magazines. These are usually painted a dull green and their new owners imagine they provide successful concealment despite

the shine from the green surface, only reduced by a cloth or net covering. The helmet is camouflaged only if it is conspicuous when seen from a short distance in open country.

Some Spandoflage pulled over a bare helmet provides a good base to work from. Spandoflage is a light stretchy material that conforms to any shape. It is available from Coxy's by mail order. Into this you can tuck small bits of weed, grass or twigs. Bracken should be used with great caution as it readily stands out against any other background. Some of the vegetation should be fixed through the front net and brought over the top of the helmet, and some weeds at the front hanging down over the shoulder give good camo effect. Remember not to do this symmetrically on both sides of the head.

This is the routine in outline, although when tried, remember to practise and test results by seeing whether you have really made your helmet invisible. Of course there are faults that you are likely to commit at first. You will put too much 'garnish' over your helmet and the result will be something more solid than the surrounding local undergrowth. You will use foliage of a different tone from that in which you wish to lie up; for example, bracken from a wood will be conspicuous in a field where there is no bracken normally. You will use over-long pieces of foliage with the result that they will wave and blow about. If you use large leaves, such as dock, they will die in a short space of time and your work will have to be done over again.

Try to think also of the changes of colour caused by changing seasons. It is wise to take a good look at a helmet wrongly garnished, as an example of what not to do. Stick a large number of bracken stems pointing upwards in the rim, so as to conceal the helmet completely. The effect will be of a bunch of bracken stems. Above all, ensure that some of the foliage sticks out of the side sufficiently to destroy the contour of the helmet where it passes over the ears, but remember to avoid interference with your sense of hearing.

The Paintball

Completed in 1982, R. P. Scherer's purpose-built Paintball encapsulation facility at Swindon was specifically designed to fulfil some quite particular need. It is equipped to the most exacting standards, and the company can offer its customers a standard of product and performance that is second to none. Product quality is vitally important to Scherer operations around the world, and the Swindon plant, built and equipped at an initial cost of £14 million with considerable further investment, is dedicated to maintaining that corporate reputation.

In mid-November 1990 the Author visited this location to see just how Britain's best Paintball ammo is made. Set in the rolling Wiltshire Downs alongside Junction 16 of the M4 Motorway and clearly visible to the passing Paintballer, it is ideally sited for ease of distribution throughout the UK and overseas. It is the only plant of its kind in Britain, and is recognized as a leader among the encapsulation industry's most sophisticated and technologically advanced plants world-wide, in the production of 'soft-gels' or soft gelatin capsules which is the technical term for the Paintball. The production departments, quality control, development laboratories, storage, service, and administration blocks occupy almost 150,000 sq ft on a 20-acre site with plenty of room for expansion.

The Paintball production side of R. P. Scherer is only the tip of a very complex iceberg. Scherer's mainstream output of soft-gels serve as efficiently designed vehicles for medicines, health and nutritional products, toiletries and veterinary formulations, and the plant produces literally billions of soft-gels for these major markets every year, handling about 1,000 different formulations.

Backed by the resources of the multi-national Scherer Corporation, the UK's R. P. Scherer Limited holds a unique position because although many of the parent company's international operations are purely pharmaceutical, the British company has developed on a broader marketing front, which is why a small but growing aspect of the Swindon facility is now engaged in Paintball production.

The first generation of British paintballs came off the Swindon line in 1984, but something makes them rather special. Scherer paintballs result from a process that is 'commercially confident'. Understandably, therefore, the company chemists will not discuss details concerning the fill formula, and the production people will not reveal the innermost secrets of the capsule's physical properties or structure. The process itself is really too complex to explain fully, despite a stage-by-stage explanation by top Scherer staff. After one and a half hours of close observation of the entire process the paintball will never again appear a 'simple' object.

The basic gelatin is sourced, usually from Europe, in granular form and like all incoming materials, is stored under quarantine conditions until it is required for processing. The term 'paintball' is something of a misnomer because it does not describe what it is that millions of enthusiasts fire at each other each week.

The Scherer ingredients include polyethylene glycol, glycerol, gelatin, water, sorbitol, opacifier, and various colourants, and even the layman can see that this is nothing like the formula for paint. As a reassurance, the formulation will not cause serious injury even if accidentally ingested in small quantities. If unlucky enough to take a mouth shot and actually swallow some of the material the advice is to rinse the mouth with copious quantities of fresh water.

Technically speaking, each paintball is a two-

▲ The paintball machine.

part system comprising the outer shell and the inner fill. The shell gives strength, shape and conformity, while the fill is a non-aqueous solution formulated to disperse the opacifier and colourant. Scherer produce both gel and fill on site, and manufacture is quality controlled from the receipt of raw materials, through quarantine storage, gel manufacture, fill manufacture, blending, encapsulation, testing and packaging. Each stage is computer recorded to identify time, date and batch, and operates so that the process is also fully retraceable throughout.

As with all the 1,000 formulations that go into Scherer soft-gels, paintballs are made using the same high-quality processing techniques which the company applies to its pharmaceutical operations. This is known within the industry as GMP, or good manufacturing practice, and as a Scherer spokesman put it: 'It is far easier to make everything to the same top bench mark of pharmaceutical GMP quality than it is

to chop and change according to product application.'

As to the actual manufacture of the paintball the heart of the process is the encapsulating machine, originally invented by Robert Pauli Scherer in the early 1930s and still unsurpassed. Into the machine are fed two flat ribbons of gelatin which pass over heated rollers and then, via a heated wedge, between a pair of rotary dies. The dies cut the two outer halves of the soft gel to shape and size — in the case of paintballs 'according to calibre' — and as the two halves are matched up, the fill is injected and the two halves are further heated and pressure sealed. This occurs in a mere fraction of the time it takes to tell. The freshly made soft-gels are then ejected from the machine on to a conveyor belt which feeds them to the wash and drier system.

The cut and discarded gelatin ribbons go into a separate system. As the paintballs drop from the machine they are soft to the touch and still warm. From the drier units they appear virtually as the user knows them, but they still have a long way to go within the process. They are now put on to large-area trays for drying time of about four days at a set temperature to remove excess moisture. After this, having reached a pre-determined hardness, they are visually inspected by skilled quality controllers who scan each batch for 'deforms' and 'leakers'. Each batch is then further random tested and if the sample is deemed unacceptable on test for any reason, the whole batch is simply destroyed.

Once a batch has passed the various stages of quality control and assurance, it is packaged in double polythene bags, boxed into outers, and weighed off. From each 'finished' batch a short sample will have been taken, just prior to sealing, for testing on the company's own firing range. The test uses a PMI paint gun firing at a plywood target from 30 metres. The test is a tough one. Any more than 3 per cent breakage in the barrel, or any less than 80 per cent breakage on target means rejection and again that means destruction of the whole batch. When you next hear a moan on site about poor quality paint, any poor results are almost certainly due to the way that the paint has been stored after it has left Scherer's control.

Scherer is not infallible and they would not claim to be: they freely admit that the odd ball may break in a box, and the very occasional imperfection

▶ *Drying paintballs.*

may slip through the net. So far, however, investigation has proved that balls that perform poorly have been improperly stored, either on-site at the club or range, or in the home. Which makes this a sensible moment to underline some facts on storage. Scherer states that paintballs should be stored in a temperature and humidity controlled environment as stated on the bulk pack outer. Where these ideal conditions are not available, the ammo should be kept at between 20 and 25 degrees Centigrade. Extremes of heat and cold above 30C and below 10C, will

adversely affect the product and given the time and care put into these soft-gels it would be a pity to ruin them out of sheer carelessness.

R. P. Scherer has invested heavily into the research and development of a British-made paintball, and most dedicated enthusiasts will probably agree that they seem to have got it right. The next five years will no doubt show more innovation in the way the sport progresses, and it is safe to assume that R. P. Scherer will be supplying the ammo used by the winning teams for many more years to come.

The Game

As with any game played for sport and pleasure there are often two levels of Paintball player; those who want enjoyment from the game itself and no more, and those who want to win at all costs.

It may be argued that to introduce 'military' tactics to the sport is to pander to the latter category of player and unncessarily complicate the game for the former who is merely out for fun. This, however, need not be the case. Already there are those who skillfully plan their games to the finest details, while others merely go out, get 'shot' and still come back smiling because they have enjoyed themselves. This will always be the case and no amount of tactical ability will change it. However, there is nothing to prevent even the most casual players from enjoying themselves, and using tactics in the process, because even the casual player likes to win occasionally and beat the more skilled opponent, thus proving his point that a Paintball game is still just a game.

Small unit tactics

For the more skilled player tactics are essential although a complicated plan of battle may not be necessary depending upon the standard of the opponents. It is also possible to create a plan so complicated that most time is taken with briefing the team and little time is left for actual play. This can spoil the enjoyment for everyone very quickly.

This section is intended to outline some basic tactics which any team can apply if they choose. Some more complicated ideas will also be examined for those who crave something extra. However nothing can ever guarantee success and much remains in the lap of the gods.

Before laying masterful plans and going too deeply into tactical deployment, it is necessary first to take account of the opposing team. If they are experienced and skilled players, an element of care is needed in dealing with them. But if the 'enemy' lacks a string of victories, meticulous planning may be totally unnecessary and the simplest plan may suffice. Furthermore, the level of skill of one's own team may not be up to intricate plans and the simple basic idea will still be best. A team with extremely clever plans can still be beaten by a team of straightforward players who have a simple plan which all of them can understand and work to.

Therefore it is useful to have a look at your enemy. If they look grim, speak in whispers and appear deep in thought they may be planning something nasty and would seem to be experts who are out to win at all costs. A very careful plan is needed to combat them it would seem. A team which appears to comprise of people out for laughs and who are smiling, joking and clowning around would give the impression that they are not terribly serious about actual victory and are out for fun, win or lose. A complicated plan is not therefore indicated.

A word of warning though; any team can put up a front before the action and can relax their opponents by pretending to be casual then become strictly professional when the game starts. Further, a team which gives the impression of being very much out for victory above all else and one from whom you might expect great cunning, may simply use the most basic tactics against you for which you have not prepared and which will then favour them with the elements of surprise. With these matters in mind it is possible before the game to confuse your enemy into totally incorrect ideas as to how you will operate, while at the same time taking stock of them and forming an opinion as to how they will act themselves. Already we have entered the realms of psychological warfare, but this need not be as daunting as it may sound. Many teams may already be practising this, perhaps even subconsciously, before a game.

Large unit tactics

A large team of perhaps twenty players offers considerable scope for dividing into several attack groups and for a variety of tactics and plans. However, it is also very easy to lose contact and control of larger groups and therefore a large team may not necessarily suit intricate tactics after all. A small team of five players is very much easier to handle although it is not possible to engage in ambitious planning because the resources are simply not there to support it. With such a team you have scope only for perhaps a two-man defence of your flag and a three-man attack. With only three men

▼ Don't bunch up close!

going on to the offensive your actual plan of battle must essentially be limited, although it will be possible for each of the three to take separate and individual routes to your objective, with the result that you have three chances of victory in that at least one of you may get through.

There is no reason why a five-man team should not defeat a twenty-man team under certain circumstances, giving rise to a considerable widening of scope for Paintball games and an increase in scenarios.

An idea for a twenty-man team deployment might be as follows. Two mutually supportive defence teams of four players each. Two independent assault teams of three men each whose task is to operate separately from the main team and seize opportunities as they arise. One six-man attack team to draw the enemy's attention and fire away from both three-man teams. This provides a powerful defence with the ability to attack in three different ways at once and using three different approaches. It does, however, mean that you will have up to five separate groups in your twenty-man team with consequent potential for chaos. This is partially reduced by allowing the two three-man assault groups a sort of 'roving commission' to operate as they think fit as the action develops. They will have a single basic task and the ability to decide for themselves how best to go about it, thus enabling a change of tactics or plans instantly to take account of unforeseen developments. Essentially they will have no particular plan at all and just a simple mission: to take the enemy flag. This relieves a great deal of complicated planning beforehand, which may all come to nothing anyway.

The eight-man defence, split into two groups, cannot operate totally independently of each other. It is possible for one group to remain around the flag while the other forms a counter-attack or reinforcement group, waiting in hiding and only coming out or engaging the enemy if the situation requires this. Alternatively they could actually allow the enemy to overcome the other defence group and then, when the enemy is withdrawing with the flag, sensing victory and moving very hurriedly with little care, ambush them when they least expect it and with every chance of knocking out the entire enemy force.

These are all possibilities based on events as they occur and represent a battle which has developed its own momentum, most probably from the overall control of the actual team leader. It closely resembles real warfare in this respect in that different groups are best given a basic task to do and left to get on with it.

It can be best, therefore, to give each group a simple and basic task to fulfil and as much leeway as they need. To ask everyone in a twenty-man team to adhere to a rigid plan, when the team might be divided into as many as five parts, is simply not going to work. The overall leader can outline his basic idea and his 'sub-unit leaders' should then fit their own tactics to accommodate it, while allowing themselves enough room to change ideas in mid-game according to the developing situation. A group taken by surprise by an enemy who is operating in an unorthodox manner is a beaten group. Yet if that group has sufficient flexibility in operating it can swiftly change its own tactics to compensate and may still win.

As a complete change, one tactic for a twenty-man team is to leave a minimal defence at the flag —

three men — and simply barrel forward in a direct line towards the enemy. No planning, no complications. A seventeen-man attack force storming forward with no intricate tactics at all, will certainly come as a surprise to an enemy who has laid careful plans against what he considered to be a careful opponent. The attack group will be large enough to overcome any enemy sub-unit it encounters since the enemy will be split into several different groups and not all of them may be encountered at all.

This is known as concentration of forces. It avoids the necessity for any planning at all and does leave the overall leader with control of all the attacking players — that is, until he gets shot himself, but even should this happen, the attack will still go forward under its own momentum without him.

▼ *Hold the tower!*

This is probably the only way in which the overall team leader can control a twenty-man team throughout the game. Without this method, he must delegate sub-leaders and trust them to do their job properly. A smaller team is obviously easier for a single leader to control throughout the game, although even an eight-man team will find occasions when the leader is out of touch with the defending or attacking sub-team. With a five-man team, the defence is left to act as best it can, while the leader is with the attackers. He will have no control over the defence and will in any case not need any, since the defence will need no direction as the game develops – there are simply not enough of them to direct. No leader's decision is necessary for the defence sub-team since their mission is simply to stay with the flag and shoot any enemy that may approach it. There are simply not enough of them to engage in clever tactical moves for which an overall leader or tactician is necessary.

In fact, a five-man team may not need a leader at all as it is small enough to dispense with overall planning and co-ordination: there is little to plan and virtually nothing to co-ordinate. Such co-ordination is only necessary when there are several sub-teams all moving with the same mission, as in a team of at least ten or twelve players.

The larger the team the greater the necessity for an overall plan, though one which can be readily adjusted to compensate for surprise moves by the enemy. Unfortunately, the larger the team and the more necessity for an overall plan, the less possibility there is for a single, overall leader actually to retain control, since the team will almost always be divided into sub-teams who will operate independently. In other words, the more the need for a leader, the harder it becomes for him to lead.

▼ *Hold the bunker!*

Whole-team tactics

Highly detailed and elaborate planning for the whole team is a waste of time since something will always go wrong, or not go according to plan. A rigid strategy which the entire team is expected to follow is not a good idea. However, there are certain ideas for a game plan such as splitting-up the attack group into three units and defence into at least two or sometimes three sub-units. The team is usually divided into defence and attack groups, both of which have clear-cut and simple tasks to carry out. This need not always be the case depending on the number of players available. There may be a flag-group to guard the flag at the exclusion of all else, a mobile defence group to intercept and ambush any enemy moving towards the flag, or to counter-attack if the flag-group appears to have been overrun. The mobile group could patrol an area anywhere within a couple of hundred yards of the flag, and set up ambushes, traps and delay snipers anywhere within it. Defence need not be simply hanging on to the flag and shooting at anyone who comes near it; it can also be a roving defence which acts rather than reacts, which certainly makes defence a more interesting mission. The attack group need not necessarily be the rest of the team or those not actually on the defensive.

With a large team, four to five members of the attack group may be 'flag-snatchers' who avoid combat until they get the chance at the flag. They could well take a different route forward to the rest of the attack-group, whose task is to bring the enemy attack-group to battle and occupy them while the 'flag-snatchers' proceed unnoticed. With a large team the attack-group may be twelve or more players and this could allow a three-pronged attack, with two groups of flag-snatchers moving ahead of the flanks while the remainder, perhaps six players, move up the centre of the site to engage the enemy attack-group. If this works the flag-snatchers could outflank the enemy and take the flag from the rear. Alternatively there is no reason why the attack-group should not be split into several individual teams of two or three men each, all making their own way to the objective to link up once more and assault the enemy flag *en masse*. With a twelve-man attack-group, this would create up to six such groups and at least half of them should get through. This requires a rendezvous near the enemy flag for all the teams who get through, where they can link up before the final assault.

The rules sometimes allow the booby-trapping of the flag so its removal triggers off a host of paint-mines. If so, this will allow the deployment of fewer men on the defence than would otherwise be necessary. In fact, a twenty-man team could leave only three snipers in the vicinity of the flag and have seventeen available for attack. The weapon-mix also dictates the tactics available to the team; especially the number of balls which can be fired before reloading. Heavy firepower is useful in the final assault on the enemy flag, while small-capacity weapons can be quite sufficient for snipers firing only one or two shots before disengaging, thus giving valuable reloading time. Small weapons such as pistols are also best for the final assault because one-handed firing allows a hand free for the flag itself.

Anything like a Tippmann SMG or similar Paintball machine-gun is strictly a defensive or support weapon. A machine-gun in the attack-group means the remainder of the group is bound to protect them because the machine-gun is too valuable a weapon to lose. Anything capable of longer than average range needs a good field of fire to realize its full potential and so restricts tactical mobility.

In very close country or when clearing a building or trench, the small, easily handled weapons are best owing to their manoeuvrability in a confined space. A sniper regularly hidden may choose such a weapon for similar reasons.

Briefing

A complicated and rigid plan to which all team-members are expected to adhere is not going to work unless the enemy has an equally rigid plan and you know every single detail of it beforehand — a somewhat unlikely event.

Further, a rigid plan will ruin everything for one's own players, particularly when they see the plan falling apart and are unable to do anything to save it because they have been strictly forbidden to deviate from it, despite any surprise move by the enemy. At the briefing then, and assuming one's team is sufficiently large to merit such a briefing, the overall plan is laid before everyone in the team. It is essentially a fluid plan with few frills and in outline only. It will take into account the likely tactics of the

▲ Slipping through the bracken.

enemy, bearing in mind the enemy's probable know-
ledge of tactics used in games on that particular site
on previous occasions. It will cover the basic missions
of any sub-teams, such as whether they are decoys
or whether they are to hold back from the main battle
and strike only if they see a good opportunity arising
as the game progresses. It will cover any change in
the team's usual tactics, since a team should change
its normal tactics frequently so as to prevent an
enemy becoming familiar with its *modus operandi*
and thereby defeating it.

It will make sure that every player knows
exactly what his particular sub-team is supposed to
do and that he/she understands their own role within
that sub-team. For example one group is a roving
group which will run interference anywhere on the
field, either to help the attack or the defence, as need
be. Or one group will keep well out of any contact
with the enemy because, 'We don't want him to

know you're there. Your job is to get in quick and get
that flag. The rest of us will draw enemy attention
from you.' As to how each group actually does get in
quick and get that flag will be up to your group when
it is finally in position to make such a move, since you
cannot know until you get there whether there will
be two enemy players defending it or ten.

All that a player needs to know, therefore, is the
particular mission allocated to his own particular
group. The briefing covers the basic way the game is
intended to be played, either a complicated plan or
simple, mass, shock-tactics. As long as each player
knows his/her or their sub-teams' part in the overall
scheme of things, they will be able to follow the basic
plan. There is nothing at all to gain by trying to get
every player to stick rigidly to a very precise strategy
since it will not work. Fine detail is left to the sub-
teams themselves. They know what they are supposed to do and will work out how to do it according
to circumstances as they arise. A briefing need only
last about five minutes, therefore, and is only to
outline the basic essentials of the team plan. Sub-

▲ *Lookouts open fire.*

teams will plan for themselves as they go along, keeping their particular mission in mind. In this way when the overall team leader looses contact and therefore control. he will at least know that the sub-team is sticking to the basic idea within its own tactical situation and therefore everything is still going according to the original plan so far as is possible.

Game drills

Every team will need to have these drills to have any chance of success in Paintball, so as to respond instantly to any surprise. At all times, for example, any group whose task it is to move forward on the attack must have a rallying point to which each player can make if the group is split up. This is the regrouping point which may be used after a successful attack, and a group must be aware as to which point is applicable, especially if there are several designated along a lengthy approach to a target.

The Army calls these RV points. On approach to a target of maybe one thousand yards, two or three RVs may be designated. The first might be one's own flag, since if one is ambushed close to one's start-point, one's flag is clearly in danger and the defence must be reinforced. After about 250 to 300 yards out, a second RV might be designated, with a third at 600 yards and a fourth just before the final attack on the enemy flag.

If taking the enemy flag does not itself mean victory and you have to return with it to your base, an RV immediately after the assault is necessary, with others on the route back. Depending upon where he is, each player must know which RV applies to his location and if the group is forced to scatter by an ambush, for instance, he/she should automatically make for that RV.

Automatic reaction is the key to good 'battle-drill'. There should be a standard recognized procedure for a range of possible incidents. For example, if you run into an ambush the worst thing you can do is mill about in the middle of it. In most cases, when you come under fire you should immediately hit the deck, but if caught in an ambush this only leaves you trapped in the middle of it to be finished off at the enemy's leisure. Anti-ambush drill is therefore one battle-drill which every player should know about so that reactions are instantaneous.

One of the best tactics to employ as soon as you are ambushed is to attack it from within, rather than try to run back the way you have come as this may lead into another ambush laid for just that purpose. It is often better to swing round and charge straight at the ambush team as fast as possible, firing like mad. This turns the ambush into a straight charge against a defended position, and of course a moving target is harder to hit. No one can claim this works every time because it doesn't, but it does work surprisingly frequently.

Upon springing an ambush, everyone should react immediately without thinking and instantly assault the ambush team. This can be practised until everyone reacts at once. Another tactic in the same situation is to have half your force immediately attack to the left and the other half to the right, especially if ambushed from both sides, though it does not matter if it turns out to be a one-sided ambush since those who have attacked in the wrong direction will find that they are able to get away and regroup while the others engage the enemy in order to give them time. A double-sided ambush should not be employed, but this does not mean your enemey will not do so. Whichever anti-ambush drill is to be used, it should be an automatic reaction by all players immediately the ambush opens fire. This can be altered accordingly upon word of command from anyone, probably the first who realizes an ambush is in progress – such as 'Ambush left!' (all attack left) or 'Ambush right!' or 'Ambush ahead!' In any ambush situation all players' reaction should be the same and immediate.

An encounter battle, such as when two opposing groups of attackers accidently bump into each other on their way to their respective targets, will also require some form of immediate drill to be carried out automatically. One such is for the leading two or three men immediately to go down and engage the enemy head on, while the remainder spread out to

either side and attempt to circle round and hit the enemy group from the flanks. Alternatively, the men at the rear may simply move aside and take up ambush positions while the two or three at the front fire a few shots and then withdraw between the rest of the team, provoking the enemy into following them – right into the hastily formed ambush. The first of these tactics is the best of the two for open terrain, while the second is the best for close terrain such as woodland.

House-clearing is similarly covered in this section. This drill is for entering a building at speed and ejecting the enemy from it. At the time of writing there are a few Paintball sites that have full-scale houses and other buildings where this drill might be necessary, but both drills are simplified to a form likely to be applicable.

We have already looked at action on the objective, where the flag is taken by a sweep through rather than attack into the objective, but there will probably be other defence locations such as trenches, sandbag outposts or similar small fortifications which, if they cannot be by-passed and made useless, will have to be cleared. The three-man group is best for this, especially if paint-grenades are available and are allowed to be used. One player is responsible for the grenade and the other two are there to guard him as he goes about his task and they stay right with him.

Throughout the manoeuvre, any other friendly players will provide covering fire as these three approach to within grenade range. The drill is not to burst into a building or defence post as seen in numerous films. This is certain to cause chaos and always means that in doing so one trusts entirely to luck and thus loses control of the attack. If we assume a six-man attacking group, then three of these become the grenade group and the remaining three the cover group. The job of the cover group is to go to earth and provide covering fire as the grenade group rushes at the objective. Any enemy players who appear at a window or stick their head up during the manoeuvre are a target for the cover group as they prevent defensive fire from engaging the grenade group.

Once at the objective; be it a window, wall or a sandbag parapet, the grenadier lobs a paint-grenade or two into the target while his two guards provide immediate cover should anyone try to interfere. Close up against a wall, anyone who wishes to interfere will have to expose a large part of himself in any case and will become an easy target for the covering group. Once the grenade has done its job, the grenade-group does not barge into the target and blast away at all and sundry. This should never be necessary as all the defenders should now have been 'hit' if the grenadier has done his job properly in the placement of his grenades. On most such occasions, the target is now out of the game and can be passed. Some sites have set rules such as all players are deemed out if in any room that receives a grenade hit even if they are not actually hit by any paint. It is best to check on this rule before the game.

A trench is possibly the most difficult target to attack in this way as the grenade-group will be exposed even as the grenades go in and a trench may require to or three grenades spaced evenly along its length. The grenade-group must therefore spend a greater period of time in the grenade range of the target, and therefore in range of defensive fire.

In this case the cover group and the two guards have to work hard and be especially alert. Equally, a trench can be difficult to get out of in a hurry without exposing oneself to covering fire. Trench defenders will be desperate to defeat the attack by jumping up and firing like mad at the grenade-group, thereby making themselves easier targets. A good grenade-group should practise this maneouvre until the action is automatic upon encountering such a defensive position. Without any orders or discussion the cover group immediately go down and provide covering fire while the grenade-group launches its attack on the run. To pause and consider the problem is to lose the momentum of the assault and it gives the enemy team time to regroup and reinforce. Speed of manoeuvre is essential once battle has been joined. Leap-frogging once in close contact with the enemy or when combat is imminent, is the best method to use when moving forward or when withdrawing under fire. Most players will already know what this means, but it still does not always work quite as it should when put in to practice.

Essentially, only half the group will be on their feet and moving at any time, while the other half is providing them with covering fire. What usually goes wrong is that the half that is moving tends to try to keep with the covering group instead of going on past them and at the very least this will provide the enemy with an excellent target for a couple of well-placed grenades. It is essential that everyone understand that the group that is moving must carry on past the covering group as the advance or withdrawal will go much more quickly. It is also important to make sure that everyone in the group knows to which half he/she belongs under such circumstances and it is obviously easier if the movement is already in staggered formation; already split into two halves with one slightly forward of the other.

Imagine two groups of four out of an eight-man attack team. One group is perhaps 25 yards ahead of the other and encounters opposition which forces it to go to ground. The second group does not charge forward 25 yards to meet up with and reinforce the first group, but moves 50 or 25 yards beyond the first group who engage the enemy and provide covering fire for this 'leap-frog'. Once the dash by the second group is completed, it is their turn to go to ground and provide cover for the move of the first group who will also go beyond by 25 yards, and so on. It helps if there is plenty of cover along the route to leap-frog into, by going from cover to cover as one moves and if so, while a group is providing covering fire for a moving group, they should have designated the cover to which they will head when it is their turn to get up and run, so that each knows exactly where to go before actually getting up. However, if there is no cover at all on the route, this method still works and may in fact be the only method that is safe and sensible to use, especially in a withdrawal.

Accurate fire is best from a static position and it is far better to have half the group actually down while providing covering fire. If everyone is up and running at the same time, accurate fire is impossible and only the static enemy, maybe defending a trench, will be able to fire with any degree of accuracy. If similarly accurate fire is coming at them from a covering group, they are more likely to keep their heads down apart from the occasional wild shot at a target which is unsafe even to contemplate. All these are drills which should become second nature to all team members.

A group that is on the move should always be split into two parts and each player should know which part he/she belongs to at all times. All these drills necessitate the group splitting up and it is vital that each player knows in which direction to go and with which half of the team. These halves can be designated number one group and number two group and if this is rehearsed so everyone knows the appropriate drill and their part in it, there is no

▶ *A two-woman sub-team moves through the undergrowth.*

reason why an alert team should suffer unduly by being surprised. If the drill is carried out correctly and without hesitation, it is the enemy team who will find themselves taken by surprise.

Immediate Action Drills

Once you are picked as a full team member on a regular team, the idea of running around in ever-decreasing circles firing at everything that moves becomes a thing of the past.

After your first two or three games, tactics begin to become a consideration. A typical example might be this. The thick undergrowth is clouded in mist as you approach your designated target, but the snap of a dead branch gives away your position and within a few seconds the quiet woodland becomes a killing ground as the ambush breaks. The undergrowth itself becomes coloured by a hail of paintballs and your team faces annihilation. Your leader has two options: remain in the hail of fire, or guide the team to turn the situation to his advantage. Study of game sites around the world shows that the best teams have a solid leader, and a basic plan of action for given situations. This is where Immediate Action Drills come in. IADs give the immediate advantage of knowing what to do and in a Paintball fight can turn defeat into victory.

Team drill nights

When part of a team and taking Paintballing slightly more seriously, it is a good idea to have team drill sessions between proper games.

The first thing is to work out some Immediate Action Drills and it is up to the team leader to ensure that plans are kept simple enough for the most inexperienced member of the team to understand. Whatever plan is used must be rehearsed over and over again because many players go to pieces when they first come under fire. The team leader must train the team to regroup and retaliate under such conditions.

Armed forces experience has proved that this type of training of repeated rehearsals builds confidence and blends the players into a finely honed team, able to deal with most contingencies. For players to work as a team requires effective communication, and precise clear and simple commands relay the information best. This can be via hand signals or verbally, but practice and rehearsal is vital to make it all second nature. Each team member must know exactly what each signal or command means; it is no good using a hand signal that is unintelligible to the rest of the team.

On parade grounds world-wide, soldiers learn drill through repetition and something similar should take place with Paintball teams. No matter how dull this may sound, the rest of the team will thank you for its when you next play and come under heavy fire. Think back to the last game that you lost and replay the game to analyse what went wrong. Put together an IAD to rectify the mistakes and rehearse until familiarity will ensure that if a similar situation arise in a future game, your team is the one that will come out on top. A selection of IAD Hand Signals that should be decided upon and rehearsed.

A Close on me.
B Halt.
C Double.
D Advance/or follow me.
E Attack.
F Slow down.
G Lie down.
H Extended line.
I Arrowhead (front view).
J Arrowhead (side view).
K Left-hand flanking.
L Move up.
M Go back/or turn around.
N Single file.
O As you were.
P No enemy in sight or suspected.
Q Enemy seen or suspected.

Approach to the flag

In your final approach to the flag, avoid the obvious and direct route if at all possible, since this will be well covered by the enemy, possibly with an ambush or trip-wires to set off anti-personnel paint-mines. The least obvious route is always the best, but an alert and tactical-minded enemy will probably expect you to take the least likely route and may watch this as well.

Since you will not wish to alert the defences the best approach will make the maximum use of cover, although it should bring you as close to the enemy flag as possible and preferably with a short and easy run in for the final assault. It may be necessary to balance a shorter run over difficult ground against a longer run over easier ground for your final assault and once you have made your choice your approach should bring you out at a jump-off point from which the assault is to be launched. The final assault is very important and it must be conducted at maximum speed for a surprise effect. Therefore the approach is not so much to the flag itself as to the point from which the assault will proceed most quickly and effectively.

Scenarios

Paintball is a sport that allows changes from the game plan in order to vary interest and to enhance skills. This is sometimes necessary to maintain the interest of the more experienced players.

A five-man team can face a twenty-man team on an escape and evasion exercise, where the five men start at one end of the site and have to reach the opposite end without being hit. This certainly improves the stalking and movement skills of the five-man team and members of this team might even set off individually as one-man escapers to prolong the game.

Alternatively, a twenty-man team might defend woodland in which there is a 'vital' installation. It will be the task of the enemy team to get through the

I.A.D. Hand
Signals

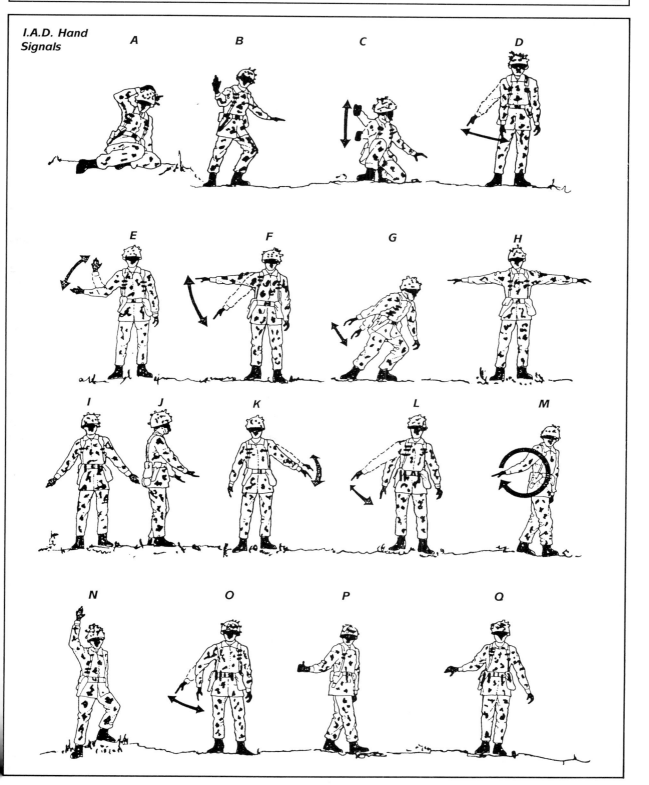

◀ *Breaking cover.*

◀ *Under heavy fire and snatching the flag.*

▶ *The flag captured.*

defence and 'blow up' the installation with paint-grenades. This can develop into another escape exercise if the installation is successfully destroyed, and points can be awarded for getting a player actually into the installation and destroying it, and for each player who successfully returns to a pre-arranged location.

A cordon and search operation by a larger team against a smaller one would resemble a professional anti-terrorist exercise, where a small, but highly skilled and experienced team faces a larger team in any of the above or some other type of scenario. In fact there is no tactical reason why opposing teams have to have the same numerical strength. After all, a twenty-man team with a couple of members who have to drop out does not have to lose three more men to take on a fifteen-man team for the sake of equality.

There is almost no limit to the scenarios which are possible if only a little imagination is applied. As the Paintball scene expands still further, there will be more and more variations on the original theme and this can only serve to maintain the increase in interest and enjoyment which the sport offers to all.

In examining individual and team tactics it has become clear that they are applicable to most Paintball games and all sizes of team. Clearly the smallest team will have to scale down some of the ideas, while the larger teams may be able to enlarge upon some of them. It is not the intention to cover every possible tactical aspect of the game, but rather the basics so as to encourage the imagination. The more experienced players may have found something of value in the tactics and ideas examined, while the new player should not be deterred by the apparent complexity of ideas and tactical considerations involved. Instead the newcomer should take note of some of the tactics and try to put them into operation in his games. In this way it is possible that the novice will gain experience and skill more rapidly than simply learning by mistakes.

To recap on the earlier ideas and plans of this section, the key-word of all these tactics must be simplicity. All tactics work best if they are kept to a level where the least experienced novice can easily remember his role. Try not to go over the top in over-organizing at the team briefing, as once the action starts a team of novice players will have forgotten most of the plan. An example of a simple brief would be to have a team of twenty. At the brief some players will not be happy in the position of fast attacking unit and these then become a natural defence unit. This leaves three squads of six men who will form the team attack force. Each player is important in pushing forward to eliminate the opponent's attack group and then continue to wipe out any defence guarding the flag. As the best plans are the simple ones each squad has a code letter:

'L' Squad, 'C' Squad, and 'R' Squad is a basic code, so simple that everyone can work it. 'L' goes left, 'C' goes up the centre and 'R' goes right. In a very basic game plan such as this, it is best to keep your players in units, because sending untrained team members out as snipers is a waste of unit firepower. Worse still they often get taken out very early in the game. A mass of unit firepower is far more lethal to the enemy team than the hope that one lone infiltrator may capture the flag.

Each unit must know that team-work with luck will work the best. At the brief each unit must remember these points above all others:

1 Do not fall behind; your team needs you up front with your gun, your eyes and ears.

2 Keep talking to your team-mates as how else will you know where the enemy is, and what you and your team are going to do.

3 Spread out to avoid clumping together. Being close may make you feel safe, but it is only an illusion: if you bunch up the enemy team will pick you all off very rapidly.

4 Once the action starts press your attack home, move fast and keep changing positions to keep the enemy confused. If the enemy fall back and outflank you, get after them and take them out a.s.a.p. Don't give them time to think, and keep them confused.

5 At some time or other, every player will find himself alone, and it feels bad the first time it happens. If pinned down the choice is to fire until your team-mates come in and rescue you or to shoot it out until some one is hit. A shootout situation is fine as long as you stay calm and pick your shots. The alternative is to fire wildly and make a lot of noise and really lay the paint down – something will happen.

If pinned down behind a tree trunk or sand bank, it is no use adopting the ideas portrayed on TV. The super hero syndrome does not work and popping up and down loosing of a few shots each time has only one outcome: an experienced player will spot you doing this stunt and the next time you pop up he'll take you out. One final point: try to vary your approach at all times even when pinned down, or you'll soon be walking back to the safe-zone because the opponents knew your movements almost before you made them.

Terrain

The type of terrain over which the game is to be played will dictate the type of tactics used. In close or wooded country there is little room to spread out and although paths will be watched by the enemy they will still tend to dictate the direction of movement. In open country with small fields and hedgerows, there is scope for wider deployment and for movement along different routes.

In woodland, movement is necessarily slow and cautious, since an ambush may lie undetected until it is too late: the enemy may be only a few feet away. More open country allows more rapid movement and in some cases may actually dictate it; with large, open spaces to cross it is inadvisable to hang around. If you know the area well, perhaps from previous games there, you will be aware as to what tactics tend to work well within it.

With open spaces, where an enemy can be seen at a distance, even while not in range, you can deploy readily against him, as long as he cannot see you doing so. Open spaces can favour the defence since an attack may be seen coming in, while woodland can actually favour the attack and enable a covered approach to the flag which ends in a sudden thrust from very close range.

Woodland has its compensations, though, in that it can channel movement along certain routes which then makes ambush easier to effect. Equally, an open area can also be of disadvantage to the defence since it will be easier to see and therefore easier to plan different approaches to it, which may be from any of a number of directions. This is not so easy to do in close woodland or undergrowth. Terrain is therefore neutral and either variety can have both advantages and disadvantages so it is important to be aware of them. A defence in woodland may only have two or three approaches to watch, since any attempt to get near by not using the paths will probably make a lot of noise and will be detected. A defence in open fields can be approached much more easily, but the defenders have a better chance of detecting such an approach. Woodland with no form of undergrowth not only allows any direction of approach, but also allows such an approach under cover.

► *The woods.*

▼ *The sand dunes.*

▲ *In the water.*

Defence is most difficult, therefore, when surrounded by trees in woodland which does not have undergrowth on its floor, to channel movements along paths. Woodland means close-quarter battle, with surprise engagements being the most frequent, while every open terrain means being able to see the enemy before he is in range and deploying accordingly to counter him, safely out of his range.

Clearly this is only the general effect and things don't always work that way, for one reason or another, but a set-piece, carefully planned and controlled battle is impossible in thick woodland or broken terrain and only rarely possible in open terrain. So even when you can see the enemy and what he is doing, luck still plays an important part in the outcome. Terrain is also clearly important as regards how much cover it provides. The old Army maxim that cover from view is not necessarily cover from fire, may still hold true for Paintball games, especially if the rules are such that you can be knocked out by only a splash of paint.

For example, if a direct hit is required before a player is classed out, then a thin hedge is cover from fire even though the target can be seen, since the folliage may well burst the paintball before it strikes

– hence the hedge does provide cover. However, if the ricochet rule is used or if only a small spot of paint is considered to class-out a player, the same thin hedge can become a liability when the ball bursts since its paint is then scattered in different directions, making a hit of some sort all the more likely. Even if the cover does protect from both view and from fire, it is not much use if you were seen getting there because you can then be pinned down behind it. After all, you have to leave cover some time and the enemy will be watching for you to do just that.

Isolated cover

Isolated cover such as a fallen log in the middle of a field can be a trap. You may gain cover quite safely, but if you were seen getting there the enemy can hold you pinned down and unable to break away while sending other players around to catch you in the crossfire. If this happens, you will need cover on all sides instead of on the one, and you will be trapped. Isolated cover which has no covered escape route or which cannot be got out of as quickly and as easily as you got in, can lead to problems.

The essence of combat is to get within range of your enemy and shoot him before he shoots you. This means approaching from a direction which he does not expect since there is no point in getting within range only to burst forward straight into a salvo of paint because he saw you approach and was perfectly ready for you.

Alternatively, if he knows exactly which direction you will come from and then watches that direction to the exclusion of all others, there is a chance for a second surprise attack from another direction. For the defence, this means that everyone must watch out in all directions. Just because they know an attack is going to come from the east, they should not all watch that direction alone, but should maintain all-round observation.

A clear field of fire in all directions, at least within range of weapons in use, is very valuable for the defence since no attack can get within range without being seen. But defence in close country is also possible because ambush of the attack is easier and a surprise attack from very close quarters is more likely to make for a successful ambush. In open country, it does not really matter if the flag can be seen because you can defend it in all directions and engage the attackers as soon as they are within maximum range. In close country it is better not to be seen until you are close enough to ambush the attackers. Therefore, in open country the defence can safely and wisely be in an obvious location, while in close country, such as thick woodland, it is better for the defence to remain hidden in ambush and to engage the enemy at close quarters, such as with a two-man team on every approach to the flag. Close country means a larger defence group, perhaps spread out to cover all approaches to the flag and with only one player or even no one at all at the flag itself. In open country, where the flag cannot be approached by surprise from any direction, a smaller defence group may be employed, all actually right with the flag itself.

In any game plan terrain will dictate operations for both the attack and the defence, so its effect should be given great consideration before anything else. The weather can also play a part in the use of terrain. A long dry spell means that every twig on the ground will snap underfoot and dry leaves will rustle.

▲ *The tower.*

This means that an attack through woodland will necessarily be slow and cautious lest it be heard. Such an attack might even be disregarded altogether because of this. Heavy rain the night before the game will soften twigs and leaves making quieter movement through woodland more easy. But, rain means mud and mud means noise as you plough through it. In prolonged dry weather, the defence is at an advantage since any approach will be heard. Under these conditions, the defence might prefer a woodland location instead of an open field. In wet conditions an open site might be better for the defence since a muddy field is difficult to cross hurriedly while going into attack and the defence has more time to pick off the attacker.

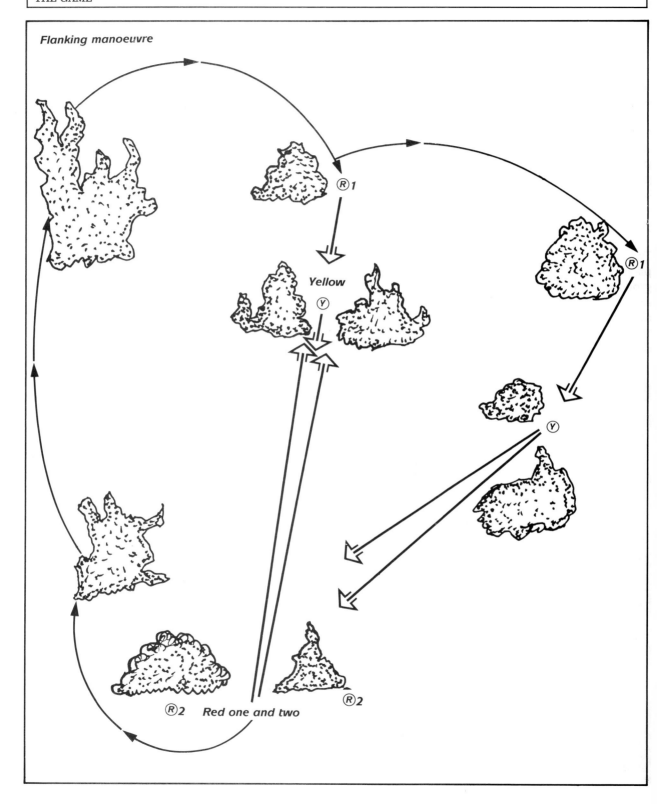

Flanking manoeuvre

Yellow

Red one and two

Flanking

As a most basic strategy, it is always a good idea to have two or more of your players automatically break away at the very start of the game to outflank the enemy team as soon as there is an engagement. The basic tactic of flanking is simply to hit the opposing team from both sides simultaneously. Novice players and teams assume that at the start of the game any player in front of you is the enemy, but as the game goes on be aware that the target in front of you may be one of your own team. Another point to remember is to watch out for enemy players creeping up behind you.

The illustration shows a very basic flanking tip: Two red players are under fire from two yellow players, both behind two separate clumps of undergrowth. One red player continues firing and the other makes his way behind both yellow players and 'takes them out' one by one. It is important for red (2) to lay down heavy fire and move into position as he does so to make yellow think that there are still two

reds pinned down. Like all play tactics the more you get used to this tactic the more effective its use will be. The flanking tactics can be used regardless of how many there are on the team, but of course the more players there are, the greater the effectiveness of the technique.

Rapid movement

If the enemy team has been spotted, surprise is just as important as speed. If it means going 30 yards more than necessary but you can keep under cover all the way, then you will undoubtedly be justified in taking the slightly longer journey. In all games there is a certain amount of risk because the enemy team does not know the exact direction of your attack, but the best route will be the one which will take you rapidly towards them and their flag while maintaining an element of surprise.

Try to avoid the mistake of starting off at a sprint. Initially there is time for thinking and decisions about the attack. No time need be wasted by the team leader or the team in thinking up their job, because the brief should have mentally prepared them to move off directly the enemy team is sighted.

▼ *Undergrowth gives cover to a two-man sub-team.*

▲ Breaking cover and making the final push.

◀ Evening ambush: good face camo and gloves.

► The marshal ensures fair play while a tower complex is stormed.

Physically it is not wise to start off at full speed. You will be thinking about what you are going to do, you will be excited and will therefore tend to be holding your breath. In a very few yards you will be out of breath and probably winded.

It is best to keep your body still and relaxed while deciding on the route to be taken, and then to start off at a gentle jog so if you have to make a sudden change of plan you will be able to accommodate the new pace. Once you have got going you can increase the pace, but the team leader must give the team full warning when the lie of the land makes him slow down, so that they in turn do not have to slow down too violently. Always remember that when you reach the other end of your run you have to be in a physical condition to fire your weapon and take-out the enemy.

Open spaces, tracks and alleyways are greater problems for the team than the safety of the cover of the fields and woodlands. Paintball in an urban setting is a different game from the woodland setting; it is much more demanding and team work is essential. Often the team will find themselves pinned down by fire from the enemy team in an urban scenario. To get the team out of this situation requires a tactic such as this.

If six players are trapped behind a wall and the only way out is past a gap, the team leader instructs the team to get across the gap one after the other at even distances as fast as they can. The first and probably the second player will get across the gap unharmed. The remaining four will get the fire intended for the first two, as well as some intended for themselves. The lesson of this is that when moving rapidly, particularly across gaps, you must not move at even distances or at too few paces from the player ahead of you. If you move at even distances the enemy players will continue to fire in a known time interval, while too close to the player in front brings the danger of sharing the paint meant for him.

The best procedure is to cross the gap as a group. Once the team is ready the leader gives the word and all dash together. This way the enemy team will have no warning. Careful team training in movement and spacing is essential in street fighting. The most common mistake made by players in this position is to hesitate as the order is given: nine times out of ten the player who hesitates is the one the enemy splat.

Night games

At some time you will probably have the chance of playing a game at night. The technique of observation at night has to be learnt as the eye functions differently at night from during the day. This is because the retina comprises two sets of cells having cones mostly in the centre, which are used in daylight, and rods grouped around the centre cones, and these are used during the hours of darkness. The cones need strong light to enable the eye to see. They will work in moonlight but under poorer conditions they are less effective. The rods are very sensitive to light and will function when the cones no longer do so. The rods are not normally used in daylight, since when looking directly at something by day the light entering the eye strikes the cones only. Everyone has the ability to see in the dark whether their day vision is perfect or not, but constant practise greatly improves night vision.

Night adaptation is the changeover from vision with the day cells in strong light to vision with the night cells in darkness. It is a slow process for which there is no short cut. The night cells can take about 30–45 minutes to become fully efficient. An alternative to sitting in darkness for half-an-hour waiting for this change, is to sit in red light for the same period of time. This will produce almost complete adaptation and allows work and briefing to be done during the waiting period. Red light bulbs in the safe are a help, but if any player starts waving torches about, the use of red lights will be a waste of time. The night cells are weak and tire quickly. Once adaptation has taken place it is not possible to look at objects for more than ten seconds before the vision becomes blurred. The angle of sight must thus be changed accordingly to allow the night cells to rest and recover. When night adapted, colours fade to shades of grey and movement is quickly spotted.

One tip taught to the Author while training for night exercises when in the Falklands is look up into the sky and fix the eyes on a fairly faint star. Without moving the centre of vision off that star, note at some distance to it a still fainter star. Then switch the focus from the first star to the fainter one. It will immediately disappear. Look back at the first star, and you will see the fainter one again. The reason for this is that part of the eye used to focus on an object is not capable of distinguishing very faint objects as parts of the eye off-centre can. If, therefore, you are not quite certain whether you can see a man moving away or coming nearer, look away a few degrees to the left or right. If your suspicions are correct you will see the faint object much more clearly.

The first time you play a night game you will find that even if played on a known site it will be very different from one played in daylight. Small, fallen branches increase in size and in the dark they appear as huge tree stumps. Similarly dense undergrowth seems like thick jungle. Any player plunged into darkness for the first time tends to be confused and lacks confidence. This is when a seasoned player should be available to help and guide him through their initial game. After a little practise night games soon become a lot of fun.

Snipers

This role is for the experienced player only. The use of a sniper is often a good idea, particularly if you have a member of your team who is more of a loner than a team player. The player for the job is best chosen by the team leader, and not by some eager

▼ *A sniper with an extra-long barrelled rifle and silencer.*

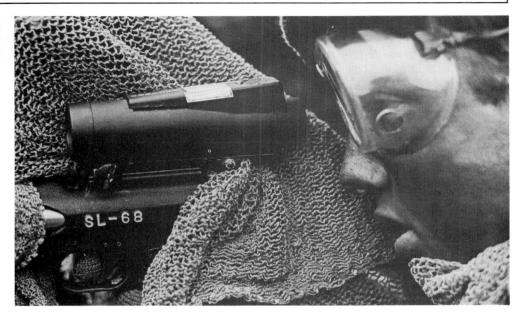

▶ *A sniper with a Cyclops sight and good woodland camo netting.*

would-be sniper. The leader can give the sniper a roving commission to wander anywhere about the game area at his own discretion and to take shots at the enemy players whenever possible. One idea could be to lurk in the general area of the flag to give support to the defence, or be sent over a long route to take the enemy flag under fire and cause maximum disruption. At best this would deplete the enemy defence before you reach it and worst could keep the defenders' heads down as you move in for the attack.

If the sniper operates mid-way along the site between both teams, delay and depletion of the enemy attack-group before it gets anywhere near your own flag is a real possibility. Essentially, the sniper is a one-man ambush, mobile and likely to spring up anywhere only to vanish and start shooting from somewhere else when least expected. A good sniper should obviously be a good shot because there is often only one chance of a shot before break off is necessary. The sniper practises fire and movement to a much greater degree than the rest of the team and given sufficient practise should become the best exponent in the team.

A sniper is always good at camouflage and concealment, but does not rely on artiicial aids such as nets since the background changes frequently and too many nets impede movement. A really good sniper can use fire and movement tactics to make the enemy believe they have run into an attack-group and spend considerable time trying to come to battle.

Your attack-group might now by-pass them and go on to assault their flag.

Sniper scope

During the past year more and more paint guns have come on to the market and a small cheap scope is available for just a few pounds. These give quite a fair performance in good daylight, enabling the average player to improve his potential quite easily. If you intend to take sniping a little more seriously, you need to dig a little deeper into your pocket. The very best rifle scopes cost hundreds of pounds as this type of scope, such as a Kahle, is designed for the user to place a bullet into big game with pinpoint accuracy at long range. This quality scope is a waste of money if put on to a standard .68 paintball gun.

Before choosing a scope it may help to know the basics of how a scope works. The scope is a set of lenses at the far or object end of the instrument which focus the image of the target through a reticule lens on to the same plane as the reticule. The image of the target and reticule is then focused by the ocular lens on to the shooter's eye, so that you see the target with the reticule superimposed on it. When you decide what size scope you are going to fit, you should bear in mind the exit pupil of the scope as this is the diameter of the focused image that reaches your eye. You can estimate this by dividing the objective lens diameter by the magnification. For

▲ The sharp end of a night sniper!

instance, a 4 × 32 scope has an exit pupil of 32 divided by 4 which equals 8mm. This is almost exactly the diameter of the human eye's pupil in poor light, so a 4 × 32 is an ideal Paintball specification.

In good light the pupil will contract to about 3mm in diameter, so there is no point in having a scope with such a large exit pupil if you only want to use it on site in broad daylight. It may look impressive to have a scope the size of a drain pipe, but small size and light weight are more valuable when it comes to actual use. A good set of mounts, and a scope that is waterproof and anti-fog are essential factors when making the final decision.

A Paintball sniper usually works at 25/40 yards, so most hits will be in the range 25 to 40 yards. Try and get as much practice as possible with your weapon in as many different terrains as possible and in all weathers, firing at targets at about this range. Lying in ambush for the enemy player or players is the best form of effective sniping with the paint gun.

Firing your paint gun with a scope fitted is far harder than might be thought because the lens of the goggles makes it very difficult to get your eye in the right position to get a full picture through the scope.

Practice will cure this problem, but however good your firing position, the cross-hairs will move slightly. Before getting too technical, remember the best shot in the world with a dubious paintball will miss the target. Unlike the high-grade rifle ammo used in combat and on competition ranges, the paintball can twist to the left or the right and even loop-the-loop so don't try and get too worried by the performance. After all Paintball is only a sport.

It is infuriating to lie waiting in a pile of stinking leaves, ready to take out an enemy player, only to find the ball breaks in the weapon. Movement to clear the jam has only one result: the enemy takes you out. It is all part of the attraction of Paintball.

Night sniper

If playing a night game there is the added problem of action under flares. If you do stumble in the under-growth and snag a trip-wire to a flare, you have only seconds to hit the deck before the overhead flare lights the sky. One point to remember is that the flare will also temporarily destroy all players' night vision so you may still have immunity for a few valuable seconds. If you are crossing a tree stump or fence when the light of the flares catches you, try to stay low and motionless until burn-out. If you are still in the game afterwards, vacate the area at all costs.

Smoke at night increases the sniper's problems; when used in wet woodlands, tall grass or reeds smoke lingers longer. When light hits the smoke it creates strange shadows and outlines change beyond recognition. If working alone make sure that it really is the enemy at whom you are aiming; night games are a new experience that has to be learnt.

The Paintball sniper is among the most deadly of the combatants in a game; moving from cover to cover, he strikes swiftly and without warning. A lone sniper can hold down sub-teams and take out vital single targets, such as the team leader. but, as for his counterpart in true combat, just as the rewards are great, so too are the risks.

Combat with an SMG-60

In fast combat on the site getting the best out of a paintball semi-auto means being totally in control of your weapon and your role. Unlike the movies, unless your target is at quite close range the weapon is best fired from the shoulder. If the target is more than 30 feet away, you can be sure that he is immune from the shot from the hip. At this range, shoulder the gun and fire a single aimed shot.

Against targets within 30 feet the weapon can be carried in an underarm assault position as you can then swing the weapon and fire as the enemy appears. Use short controlled bursts; bursts of more than five balls are often a waste of paint.

Vintage players soon learn to look through cover rather than straight at it so don't expect the enemy to pop up like a target on the range; experienced players soon learn not to turn their backs on any unchecked cover. Try to avoid getting any closer than you need because there is simply little or no advantage in getting too close to the enemy.

Even the best Paintball players cannot accurately judge how many balls they have fired in a fast fire-fight. It is therefore advisable to change the magazine after four short bursts in case you run out at a critical moment. Get under cover and top-up as quickly as possible. All Paintball weapons have a ball breakage at some time or another, but do not start to strip the weapon out in the open. Your first priority is to get under cover before attempting the malfunction drill.

Saboteur

The role of the lone saboteur is best illustrated with a personal reminiscence.

The coldness of the thigh-deep water started to take effect, and the lower half of my body went numb as I half-waded half-stumbled onward. Mist swirled along the centre of the creek. High on either bank the breeze whispered as it passed through the reeds. Holding my weapon high above the water made progress unsteady and it was difficult to keep my balance; the noise I made chilled my nerves more than the water's coldness. The straps of my back-pack cut into my shoulders and I was rapidly becoming exhausted. In the half-light the reflections from the bank on the water made me jumpy and my finger tightened on the trigger.

I stopped at the sound of voices from the bank above me. The sound increased as the enemy patrol thrashed closer. I felt sure I'd be discovered if I cocked my weapon. As I waited, the water swirled round me and I could feel sweat start to ooze on my brow and along the rims of my goggles. Wading

closer to the bank the deep mud swirled up in telltale clouds, giving away my position. My ears, amplifying every sound of movement, planted seeds of fear and triggered off an adrenalin rush.

The voices sounded much clearer; this time surely they would spot me and I waited for the sound of weapon fire, anticipating the thud of paintball on my clothes. But the search patrol moved away and once more there was silence save for the sounds of the water as it lapped against the banks.

Moving off, I rounded a bend and the water was shallower here and the light brightened to reveal a wooden bridge. Stopping for a moment I listened to make sure all was clear before resting my SL.68 on the bridge and hauling myself out. After even a short time in the water the wet and coldness had made my body feel like lead and my fingers slipped and received splinters as I pulled myself on to the woodwork. Picking up my weapon I filled the magazine and quickly checked to make sure that no mud had found its way into the barrel or mechanism.

Slipping into the cover of the dense reed bed, I slipped off my back-pack and the pain in my shoulders made me wince. Thankfully the anti-personnel paint-mines were intact and dry as I removed them from the polythene wrapping: five mines, plus batteries and masking tape, nylon quick-release detonator cord, and all the other tools of the trade. With it all in a polythene bag, I slipped my gun over my shoulder and gripping the bag in my teeth stealthily made my way back into the water.

If anything the cold was more intense than before, and made the wiring up of the charges a long job; I noticed that I'd cut my lip when I started to strip the wires with my teeth. I had to use lots of tape to secure the mines because the woodwork was soaking wet and I doubted if the tape would hold at all. I placed two mines each side so each end had a charge facing along the bridge and out on to the track in both directions. This was designed to get any player running away and splat him on the retreat. I had intended to place the fifth and final mine on the path on the far side of the bridge, but the cold was taking its toll and I dropped it into the murky water. Finally I pulled out the fine nylon quick-release detonator cords from the mines and back along under the bridge. Carefully, using a small thumb tack, I temporarily secured the cords. Taking out a tube of new paintballs I loosely wrapped the nylon round the tube, laying it flat in the centre of the bridge in full view. The weight of the tube was enough to hold the quick release detonator cords in position and arming the trip-switch I removed the thumb tack. What player could resist picking up a brand-new full tube of paint?

I quickly left the bridge and took cover in the reeds. The sound of water fowl from the creek assured me my cover was good and I lay, peering through the reeds, waiting for the enemy to break cover. Suddenly the silence was broken as the enemy appeared. Two were coming up the creek with another three snaking through the reed bed on the far side. Slowly they met on the far side of the bridge. I took aim at the largest target, but the small chances of escaping kept me from firing. Slowly the first player made his way on to the bridge; he looked right and left and appeared to look directly at me in the cover of the reeds. Slowly and cautiously he made his way over, but did not look down and passed over the trap unnoticed. Now he stood only feet away from my cover. He beckoned the other players to follow him. Within a matter of moments four of them were on the bridge. Through the silence an excited voice yelled, 'Hey Jim, look what I've found . . .' and the blast of the mines ended the sentence. The Brocks anti-personnel paint-mines had been even deadlier than usual and the players on the bridge were splatted from head to foot and looked scared to death.

Breaking cover I zapped the fifth player in the back to his total amazement. The hooter then sounded and game ended.

Later I discovered that my hits had all been first-time players. All of them worked in the sales department of a large computer firm and they had decided to give Paintball a try but had only heard about the basic, original game and not about the special training day games. As we washed up and changed, the pure thrill of the sport bubbled in their conversation and I guess that they are now playing regularly.

Trip wires, pressure pads and trigger switches

Anti-personnel paint-mines are the type of pyro that can easily be wired to use as a booby-trap. In some game scenarios a well-wired trap is as good as an extra player or two. This type of pyro however should only be used on a site where the organizers know and allow for it in the day's play. Both skill and time are required to lay a trap properly, but with a little practise it is within the scope of most players.

Trap idea A To booby-trap the flag in a wooded area all your own team must know the area, the game plan and how the mines are to be used. It is vital that every member be totally sure or you could well take out your own team-mates. An open section

◀ *A sniper waits for a target.*

of the wooded area is the best spot to place the flag. Find the main path leading to this area and on this lay a trip-wire placed so that the enemy team can see it as they approach. The instant this trip-wire is detected it will stop them in their tracks. This also gives immediate psychological advantage to your team. The flag defence should now be able to take out some of the enemy with gunfire, but remember that the trip-wire is only a dummy and has no charge.

At the same time as laying the dummy trip-wire, place three anti-personnel mines around the flag with the blast area facing the flag. The distance from the flag should be four to five feet. It is important that the wires from the mines to the battery and trigger device be well covered. Equally important is that the mines be clear of hard debris such as pebbles, rocks or hard clay as this could be hazardous on detonation.

At the base of the flag-pole fit the trigger switch and when finally in position, arm it. If the flag is moved the mines will detonate and the inward arc of the explosion will take out all the players in the explosion-zone. In the following confusion the defence should be able to remove any of remaining enemy players close at hand.

Trap idea B On some sites the terrain may have a stream or stretch of water. This may be of concern to you because the enemy team may outflank and attack your rear, slipping up behind you using the stream as cover. To deter this place four anti-personnel mines in the bank of the stream at waist level. Lay them in staggered zig-zag pattern about two feet apart, making an eight-foot run in all. It is better to lay all the mines on the same bank because the explosive effect is greater. Place the charges on the bank where the water runs shallowest because the enemy will not wade along the deep areas of the stream.

Reel out the trip-wire so that it runs under the surface of the water and about 4 to 5 inches above the stream bed; this is roughly the height to get a boot-toe to snag the wire and detonate the mines. If you lay the trip-wire flat on the stream bed the enemy will walk over it without any results. Be careful also not to run the wire too high in the water as it will cause surface activity and will be spotted. The trip-wire has to be set correctly to be fully effective. Wires from the trip-wire to the trigger device and charges can be easily hidden as most areas along streams have lush vegetation where the mines can be set in soft mud or sand.

Be sure that you do not leave foot or hand marks in the soft mud while you are wiring the charges as it will completely waste the time spent in laying the trap. A small branch with leaves can be used to mask any trace of your presence, but be very careful not to break the vegetation where the bank touches the water as this will alert the enemy that something is afoot.

Trap idea C In an area that uses both outdoor and indoor sites for urban combat, the use of pressure pads may be better as this trigger device adapts easily to use under mats, floor boards, and rubbish. The top landing of a staircase is a prime position to set a trap. Laying a trap for the first step would usually be a waste of effort as the probability of the first two steps being wired is so high that the enemy will deliberately avoid them.

For best results use masking or carpet tape to fasten two anti-personnel mines out of sight at each end of the landing, pointing in an arc covering the top section of the stairs. Around the middle of the landing put a pressure pad trigger device under an old mat or sheet of newspaper. Once armed and stood on this will trigger the mines, taking out the players on the landing and also any players at the top of the stairs. Try to avoid laying mines under old wood or builders' rubble as this could add hazardous projectiles to the explosive discharge. Never use any type of explosive pyro in a building that still has glass or part-glass in its structure.

The use of pyrotechnics adds another dimension to the excitement of Paintball but must be used only if all players know from the start that this type of item is in use. This topic will always remain a matter of personal preference, but pyros are an established part of Paintball and many players consider them a valuable extra ingredient to the sport.

The trigger device mentioned in this section can be obtained from Pyro Supplies UK. Tel: 0424 753588. The pressure pads are supplied by Electromail, Tel: 0536 204555.

Entering buildings

Some sites now have indoor and urban settings and in this type of game the following plan works quite well. But first make sure that the owners allow the use of pyros. For entering a building or room it is easier to work in pairs as this reduces the chance of shooting your own team-mates.

Player 1 moves to the door and if closed checks the hinges to see which way it opens, while player 2 covers him at all times. Never stand in front of the door because if it suddenly swings open it is a sure bet that a volley of rounds will follow. If the door is open one player tosses in a paint-grenade as will player 2 if time allows. As soon as the grenades explode both players enter the room and shoot at any enemy player visible; if possible remember to fire short bursts and aim low. As soon as the room is clear shout out to the back-up members of your team to enter the room. You must remember to wait for both grenades to explode before entering the room because there is a chance that the enemy may throw or kick out the grenades. Two grenades are better than one as it causes confusion and doubles the odds of making a definite hit.

If you have to make your way upstairs, cover is essential. One player covers the stair well as the other makes his way up the stairs. It is wise to remember the dangers of trip-wires on the stairs, or of a grenade rolling down on to you. If you decide to use another grenade it is better to go outside and see if you can toss one through a window, this being easier than trying to throw one up the stairs. Any movement above you will be the enemy and at first sight of the enemy player squeeze off a short burst at each target. In the heat of the moment you may fire a longer burst than is required just to make sure, but after training the double-pump will work better and save both time and ammo.

Make sure that when you clear a room you check out every hide-a-way so as not to leave an enemy player behind. Always check the room wall to wall including cupboards and upturned furniture and never call in your back-up team until this has been done and you are satisfied that the room is safe. Also, it is best for only one pair to work a room or building at a time as the chances of the same team shooting their own men are high.

On sites that use the grenade rule of anyone in a room or bunker classed automatically out when the grenade or mine explodes, the rules of engagement must be clear to both teams at the start of each game.

Air attack

The gentle whisper of the blades rose to a high-pitched whine as the chopper shuddered and lifted off.

The team sat grasping weapons in silence in the cabin of a troop-carrying helicopter. The noise was tremendous and every available space was jammed with essential equipment. Below were three Land-Rovers bumping their way over the plain, the flickering of red brake lights showed bright and clear from above. The chopper's engine made every loose item of kit chatter and shake, even the rings on webbing made the smoke-grenades vibrate loudly. Shortly after lift-off we were circling and making our drop and three of us quickly slipped to the ground in the wind storm of the blades, and the chopper was away. The Wiltshire countryside stood still and miles away over the plain we could make out the three Land-Rovers. Checking the map we sought the shortest route to the flag area. Bracken grew to waist height making the going slower and harder than any of us had anticipated, though we had realized our maps and aerial photographs would not reveal everything. With the aid of a small scope, we saw that the Land-Rovers had left, vanished, meaning each team was now heading for the flag.

We each had been given the chance of land or air with both teams handicapped evenly in time and distance. It just happened that Alpha team had won the toss at base and had chosen the chopper. And now the Bravo team were somewhere out on the plain, heading towards the flag. As we went on our way the bracken became thinner and changed to heather and gorse and our time picked up. Stopping on a small, sandy dune, we all had a quick bite from our rations.

On the far ridge the flag could be seen hanging limp in the silent air. Picking up our weapons, we headed off towards it as high above two Chinook helicopters passed over. Within half an hour we were slowly making our way up the ridge, two of us heading directly upwards and a third man taking a flanking route in case Bravo were closer than anticipated. The climb up the ridge was far steeper than the map had indicated, but the anti-mist on my goggles was working well and no amount of sweat could fog my vision.

Climbing over the top I nearly opened fire, but stopped just in time; two marshals were talking to each other over their radios. The Bravo team were making their way up towards the flag below us and were easily visible. In the rules of this particular game the first team to capture the flag and fire red smoke would be the winner. From where I lay, I could see the flag. I could make a dash and grab the flag, but the opposition would take me out before I could fire the smoke-grenade. The sound of semi-automatic fire broke the silence as each team thought how best to take the flag. Rolling over the edge of the ridge I opened fire, while my team mate simultaneously threw a paint-grenade. I was already diving for the flag and paint was splattering on the area around me, but I was untouched as I grabbed the flag, sat down, and fired off the red smoke-grenade. The marshal's hooter blasted, and the game was over. It had taken two hours and thirty-five minutes to capture the flag; an exhausting game. Shortly we all sat talking about the exercise and as we rested the marshals radioed for the chopper to pick up Bravo team. Alpha team had to walk down the valley to the Land-Rovers as we had agreed that if one team flew in the other team would fly back. I had really enjoyed the day and thank Twin City Enterprises for inviting me to play and report on their first test game before opening in the spring of 1991.

Encounters 'Delta Dawn'

The smell of pine trees overwhelmed the senses and the silence of the forest was deafening. The sun cut long golden shafts into the dark undergrowth as, checking the magazine of my weapon, I topped up with a few extra rounds. Now and then sounds of movement could be detected and I made my way slowly through the undergrowth, bramble and gorse tearing at my clothing.

Rolling into a bomb crater I made contact with two members of my troop. In low whispers we exchanged information on the areas reconnoitred. It became clear that we were the farthest advanced of the team and, provided that no casualties had been received, it meant that on our flank we had seven more players heading towards the objective. As we lay together in enforced proximity, the smell of pig manure steamed from our clothing: each of us had used the same ditch that ran back through the woodland from the farm. In single file we left the safety of the crater and made off through the dense bushes. There was a sudden squeal and snorting as the bushes burst open and a sow and her piglets ran through the group. Each thought we had engaged the enemy and the sound of this disturbance alone must

have given our position away. We made off in separate directions and again, not a word was said.

As I made my way forward the woodland opened up and the undergrowth petered out, giving way to a well-worn track with pine trees towering up on each side. Keeping to the edge of the track, I followed it until the bright sunlight beckoned at the rim of the forest. Cocking my weapon, I edged out into the clearing; the light seemed even brighter through the lenses of my face mask. I eased myself into position with a good view of the clearing and examined the tall structure that was our target.

The Tower rose high above the surrounding countryside and the barrel of a weapon protruded from each defence port. Camo netting cascaded down over bales of straw and within the base I could see the reflection of the sun on the goggles of the enemy team: five players were defending the base. The land around the Tower consisted of dense undergrowth broken up by deeply pitted bomb craters of various shapes and sizes. Two underground tunnels ran to one side of the Tower, but this area was known to be trip-wired. The only cover for an attack was in the craters and the gorse and heather.

The barrels in the tower trained on to the area from which a bird had broken cover, as the enemy suspected the bird had been disturbed by troop movement. Silence returned, distrubed only by the movement from the defences inside the observation Tower. Then the calm was shattered by explosions as grenades and smoke-bombs flew through the air and rounds splatted against the metal of the Tower. In the midst of all the white smoke came a burst of red smoke, the chosen signal for our all-out attack. As I stood up and broke cover, the area where I had been became heavily splatted by paintballs and I made for the Tower, following the noise of weaponry and the sound of battle. Firing on semi-automatic I was suddenly at the base of the Tower and still untouched by enemy fire. I quickly eliminated two of the enemy team immediately in front of me, but then came a jolt on my goggles and my vision turned red as I received a head shot. Before I could raise a gloved hand to wipe the splat, a thud in the chest let me know that my game was over. Walking back to the safe-zone, I could hear a cheer indicating that our team had taken the Tower and won the game.

This is the Author's account of a game he experienced at Encounters.

There is rain, and then there is rain and on that day at Encounters' site in Wiltshire, it was definitely the latter. Upon opening the large iron gate, we were on Ian and Janet Horton's site. The mud was ankle deep, vast puddles covered the car park and the area was edged by an electric fence. This was not a case of taking the 'war' scenario too far, but was to keep pigs from getting on site. Since writing all the pigs have gone. Encounters is solely a Paintball and adventure centre. Encounters started with nothing and the work put in by the staff on this family-run site has to be praised. Where once were disused farm buildings, now stands a custom-built Paintball venue with covered changing area, covered eating area with seating and tables in a large barbecue area. Male/female showers and wash-rooms together with flush toilets are on site too. The site also boasts a custom-stocked armoury filled to bursting point with state-of-the-art weaponry and every player is issued with a Constant Air System; Encounters being one of the very first sites to use it as standard issue.

First-time players can choose the type of protection they wish to wear, from fully visored helmets to the very latest goggle protection. If you intend to use your own goggles they must stand up to the safety testing procedure before being allowed on site. In this test the Author's own goggles failed the test, the goggles as used for months were in fact dangerous and luck alone had prevented serious eye injuries.

The armoury even boasts breast protection equipment for female players. The site now has one of the best Towers in the UK as well as a system of tunnels that is excellent. Radar stations and bunkers put the adventure in a class of its own.

Located in rural Wiltshire, each season gives the site a new look, and the sheer size of the place allows for a vast range of scenarios. The actual terrain varies from open woodland to dense undergrowth, and in each area bridges, ammo dumps and defence stations have been constructed. In 1990 the site had one of the first children's game day in which, under 'Very Special Conditions', with a one to one (adult/child) basis, children from the local area were given the chance to play a heavily monitored game. This was such a huge success that a repeat could well be on the books.

The Encounters site has something for everyone and is part of the new breed of independent sites that have weathered the test of time.

For full details contact: Ian and Jan Horton, Encounters, Woodside Bottom, Lords Oak, Landford, Wiltshire SP5 2DW. Tel: 0794 390590.

Female Paintballers

It was in 1989 that female players first made the print and today women think they have one choice: to be passive and feminine or to be butch man-hating Amazons. The truth is they need be neither. Paintball is a sport in which men and women compete as equals and many women are grateful to have this opportunity to dispel chauvinistic ideas of butchness or soft femininity.

Women players are often much better than the men and approach Paintball with the same intention as men do, for pure enjoyment. The days of men gazing in amusement as a woman walks on site are long gone and rightly so. The Author's wife has put up with a lot over the years. As assistant on photographic shoots, her contribution has been very helpful in pointing out the feminine angle as to which weapons and equipment are user-friendly; has probably seen more Paintball weaponry than most players. What is it however that compels top women executives, nurses, teachers, etc., to give up their weekends and days off to run wild on a Paintball field? The answer should be that their motivation is the same as for men, and when interviewed many said that the idea of dressing up in camouflage was quite a large part of the fun. But the greatest thrill was to be able to 'shoot a man': for some it was almost an erotic sensation to see the paint splat on their targets.

In mid 1989 a game by Mayhem at Battle-Zone on the outskirts of Rochester, Kent had teams with female players from a model agency. As the game got under way, the models were getting into the Paintball scene in a big way, crawling through the thick, wet woodlands and huge patches of nettles. Crawling through thick undergrowth was a far cry from the work they do every day in the studios, but they loved it. Once in battle dress and camo paint, none gave them a second glance.

As the smoke clouded the battlefield and the zap of Splatmasters and PMIs filled the air, a comment overheard confirmed the truth of the potency of the female Paintballer. In the thick of the fighting a female gave out a yell and a male voice said

► A female sub-team takes and defends a tunnel.

'Oh sorry'. The next instant a Splatmaster fired and the same male voice exclaimed, 'She shot me! I only walked over to say sorry and she's shot me.'

The lunch break illustrated the fun and excitement that these first-time players were having as nearly everyone of them said they would play the game again at a later date. There is simply no reason why more women should not play Paintball.

In mid 1988 the author covered a game on the outskirts of Harrogate, North Yorkshire at Atac-Tix. This site is managed by Carol Sutton, Tim Brewis, Richard Brewis and his wife Chris. Living at Bilton Hall Farm in an area of outstanding natural beauty, Carol, Tim and Richard determined from the start that nothing would damage the ecology of the countryside. Contacting a leading ecologist they discussed the site plan, and listened to the expert with great interest. Acting on his recommendations the site was built so as not to endanger or risk the natural flora and fauna. The famous quote from the Falklands War 'I counted them all out and I counted them all back,' could be the site motto, as no empty paintball tube or gas cartridge is left to litter up the site.

At the time of my visit, Atac-Tix had a few female players and a female marshal, proof that Paintball is just as much a female sport. It can only be to the good of the sport if more ladies grab a paint gun and join Paintball. Like Atac-Tix, there are sites the world over that are happy to see first-time female players, and Paintball is a great way of meeting the opposite sex! Couples can now play the sport together and it is not unusual to see husband and wife members of a team, and sometimes on different teams. At an Ultimate Games UK Tournament in October 1989 the Author found our more about female motivation in Paintball. The reasons again revolve around the sheer fun and excitement of Paintball and how it is a different world from that of the working week. To prove the diversity of those who take up Paintball, recruits ranged from a hairdresser to an archivist.

One of the UK's leading models of Paintball Camo Clothing revealed how sports clothing has taken a move towards designer styled sports-wear. In the nineties one-piece camo suits can be made to give protection to the female player, such as in the HockBo Arms range of jump-suits. The all in one jump-suit was specifically made for women as the suits were designed with the upper tube pouch strategically placed to protect the bust area, with extra padding to the upper body and a padded neck protector. Female players can be confident that they can avoid most bruises.

Many female players were not keen on Paintball because of hits through thin clothing causing bruises. This was a major disadvantage and caused the number of female players to fall at this time. Now the new breed of protective clothing reduces the chance of a bruise to virtually nil and all females can enjoy the sport.

Paintball Law

This section discusses law and the legislation governing Paintball. In England, Scotland and Wales the Firearms Act of 1968 covers the game. The Firearms Act (1968) is a very complex document. With regards to Paintball weaponry it is for the relevant Chief Constable to determine whether a particular weapon requires a firearm certificate and, in the final analysis, for the courts to decide whether he has acted reasonably in terms of the law. To get the very latest views on how the law stands the Author wrote to the Home Office. The Home Office letter to Mr Richard Cooke, 25 June 1991, is the most up to date authority available:

'   Dear Mr Cooke,

CO₂ POWERED PAINTBALL GUNS AND AIR WEAPONS: LEGAL STATUS

Thank you for your letter of 18th June about the legal status of paint pellet guns powered by CO_2 gas.

For a gun to be subject to control under the Firearms Acts 1968 to 1988 Act, it must comply with the definition provided for in section 57 of the 1968 Act, which is that it must be a "lethal barrelled weapon". In 1960, in the case of *Moore* v *Gooderham*, the Appeal Court ruled that "lethal" could be held to mean capable of causing an injury which might lead to death. Although only a court can give a definitive ruling as to whether any particular gun is subject to control under the Firearms Acts, we have in the past expressed an opinion, based on advice received from our technical experts, that certain of the guns used in adventure games cannot be described as lethal barrelled weapons because they are unlikely to cause an injury leading to death and are thus not subject to control.

In our view a paint pellet gun powered by CO_2 gas falls outside the definition of a firearm if:

    i.   the maximum velocity with which paint or dye pellets are discharged from the weapon does not exceed 180 feet per second (fps);

    ii.   the weapon is capable of firing only paint-pellets with which it is supplied; and

    iii.   the contents of the pellet are non-toxic. We understand that a toxic oil based paint may be regarded as a noxious substance under section 5 of the 1968 Act.

Guns which are of higher discharge velocity than 180 fps would in our view require a firearm certificate under section 1 of the 1968 Act and a gun of such a higher discharge velocity which also has a self-loading operation may be prohibited by virtue of section 5 of that Act.

It should also be noted that if any such gun has the appearance of a firearm to which section 1 of the Firearms Act 1968 applies and it is readily convertible to fire paint pellets in excess of 180 fps, then by virtue of the Firearms Act 1982 the gun would be subject to control under section 1 of the 1968 Act.

However, as I have said above, only the courts can give a definitive ruling on the status of a particular gun.   '

This section of my book does not constitute legal advice and it is advisable to consult legal counsel to determine how the law may apply to personal circumstances.

Paintball laws in the USA

As the sport is truly international it is of interest to detail how the sport is governed in America. For this information the Author is indebted to Jessica J. Sparks, the leading lady of Paintball.

J. J. Sparks, Attorney and Counsellor At Law, admitted to practice before the Bar of the State of California, the US District Courts and the Ninth Circuit Court of Appeals. J.D. 1983, University of California, Los Angeles; Board of Editors, UCLA Law Review and UCLA-Alaska Law Review. Board of Directors and Legal Counsel, International Paintball Players Association, Inc. (IPPA); a principal founder of the IPPA. For the IPPA, drafted, reviewed and revised legislation affecting Paintball in the USA and abroad. Testified before the state of California Senate Judiciary Committee. Qualified as a Paintball expert for court and zoning board testimony.

Paintball is not subject to heavy governmental regulations in the USA. Air gun or firearms law have some effect on Paintball, but not in all areas of the country. Local regulations, principally zoning laws, have the most impact on Paintball because they relate to site and sometimes storage location.

Little or no government-originated safety regulation is imposed on the sport throughout the USA, yet this lack of formal regulation has not resulted in a dangerous sport. In fact Paintball is proof of self-regulation and it remains an extremely safe sport. According to annual statistics compiled by the National Safety Council (USA) the game is safer than swimming, tennis, jogging, skiing, fishing and most other recreational activities. Field safety standards have been set by the insurance companies and the International Paintball Players Association (IPPA).

Players frequently take an active role in protecting their sport by refusing to play at fields where safety rules are not strictly enforced. Responsible manufacturers consider safety factors when marketing Paintball products, while responsible field operators and store owners will not sell or permit use of products that are unsafe for use in the sport. This all creates an enviable and excellent safety record. Here follow the major US Laws regulating Paintball. This chapter does not constitute legal advice. You are advised to consult with legal counsel in order to determine how these and other laws may apply to any specific set of facts affecting you.

The Paintball guns commonly used in the USA are carbon dioxide powered air guns. Federal law, passed by the US Congress, does not include such air guns in the classification of firearms under federal firearms statutes. Simply put, Paintball guns under federal law and, thus, the federal firearms laws, do not apply to Paintguns. Other air guns such as traditional BB-guns and pellet guns are not firearms under federal law.

Federal toy gun law Paintball guns are not 'toy' guns under federal law. Efforts by the IPPA resulted in a specific exemption for Paintball guns being written into the 1988 federal toy gun law. The law requires that each 'toy' look-alike or imitation firearm have a permanent blaze-orange barrel plug. However, the term 'look-alike firearm' explicitly does not include Paintball guns. Paintball Guns, BB and pellet guns are not required to have permanent orange barrel plugs.

Furthermore the federal toy gun law has specific provision providing additional protection for the rights of Paintball players. No state law, local law or ordinance can prohibit the sale of Paintball guns. Only their sale to minors may be prohibited.

Federal law on sound suppressors Under federal law, without a federal permit one may not possess a device, a silencer or sound suppressor capable of muffling the sound of a firearm. The Federal Bureau of Alcohol, Tobacco and Firearms (BATF) has a procedure for testing such devices. If the device is capable of silencing a firearm according to BATF standards, the device may only be possessed by those with a federal permit. Sound suppressors used in playing Paintball have been sent to BATF for testing, and nearly all have been declared illegal. If a sound suppressor is tested and BATF determines it not a silencer, BATF issues a letter, so stating to the person submitting the device for testing. That device as well as those manufactured exactly like it can be possessed or sold without a federal permit. Those who manufacture, sell or possess a non-approved device risk a felony violation of federal law.

Firearms and air gun laws of various states Paintball games operate legally in all fifty states. No state regulates Paintball guns so as to require a background check, permit or registration to purchase them. With very few exceptions, individual state firearms laws do not apply to Paintguns. No state refers to velocity of the projectile (feet per second) in defining a firearm.

In over sixty per cent of the states, a firearm is defined by its ability to propel a projectile by force of an explosion, combustion or burning. Air guns, including carbon dioxide-powered Paintguns, generate no such explosion, combustion or burning and thus are not firearms under such definitions. In states with such a definition, the firearms laws do not apply.

In some states where the definition of a firearm is very broad, the laws could be interpreted to include Paintball guns. For example, if a firearm is defined as an instrument which expels a projectile by any force including air, Paintguns are technically included in that definition. However, even in those states the IPPA is not aware of any instances in which the firearms laws have been applied to restrict the game.

The only state in which officials of the government attempted to apply existing state firearms law

to restrict Paintball was New Jersey. Until 1988, New Jersey police and other state officials had often told citizens that Paintball guns were firearms and that Paintball was an illegal activity. Paintguns had been confiscated, and fields could not run openly although Paintball was widely played on private land, sometimes with police participation.

New Jersey definition of a firearm includes air guns which expel a missile smaller than three-eighths of an inch such as BB and pellet guns and the definition of a destruction device includes weapons capable of firing a projectile greater than .60 calibre

such as rockets and Molotov cocktails. In a 1988 lawsuit against the state brought by Raymond Gong, the state argued that Paintballs of .68, .60 and .50 calibre fit the latter definition, and Paintguns are air guns even though the projectile size is greater than three-eighths of an inch. At trial in Gong's lawsuit, key testimony came from IPPA board members and technical expert Bud Orr of Worr Games Products.

The trial judge ruled that Paintball guns were neither firearms nor destructive devices under state law. That decision upheld by a unanimous court of appeals opened the fiftieth state to Paintball.

the industry generates jobs and revenue for citizens and companies in the state.

California is the only state where the definition of a firearm specifically includes Paintball guns. As of January 1st 1989, the category of firearms was expanded to include instruments which expel metallic projectiles (such as BB guns and pellet guns) and 'any spot marker gun' (Paintball gun). However, that definition was expanded to protect Paintguns and air guns from the new California toy gun law.

Testimony and efforts by the IPPA and the air gun industry resulted in this protection for all air guns. California's toy gun law defines an imitation firearm as 'a replica of a firearm which is so substantially similar in physical properties to an existing firearm as to lead a reasonable person to conclude that the replica is a firearm'. One who sells, manufactures or distributes an imitation firearm 'shall be liable for a civil fine' of not more than ten thousand dollars ($10,000) for each violation. Because air guns are 'firearms', by definition they cannot be 'imitation firearms'. Furthermore, even though air guns are generally classified as firearms, they are exempt from most California firearms laws. For example, firearms laws which do not apply are laws requiring firearms registration and a waiting period for firearms purchase, and the law prohibiting the carrying of a loaded firearm. None of the laws regulating firearms 'capable of being concealed upon the person' apply.

In a related case in California, a Paintball player discharged his Paintgun at his goggles on the ground in an alley. A neighbour looked out of the window, saw the Paintgun and called the police. The police arrested the player for brandishing a toy gun. Although the police incorrectly charged the player, since the Paintgun was not a toy gun under the new California firearms law and he had not brandished it at anyone, the player still suffered considerable distress from the arrest. He also lost his Paintgun until the charges were dropped and an IPPA attorney secured it back from the police.

To avoid such situations, players are advised never to carry their Paintguns uncovered when in public, and never to discharge their Paintguns where such a problem can arise.

In Illinois, a 1989 law establishes a separate legal classification for Paintguns; a similar law is under consideration in another state. Such laws place

▲ *A woodland attack.*

Since the ruling, fields and stores have opened throughout New Jersey. No state restricts Paintgun possession by adults. In 1988, a bill was proposed in Illinois that would have prohibited possession of Paintball guns throughout the state. However, efforts by the IPPA and Illinois Paintball supporters caused legislators to drop the bill. The legislators came to understand that the game is a safe form of adult recreation enjoyed by law-abiding citizens, and that

Paintball guns in a category of their own, completely distinct from firearms and toy guns. Having Paintguns in their own category, as a special type of sporting gun, can prevent erroneous or unjustified misapplication of other laws to the detriment of Paintball players and the Paintball industry.

State laws affecting minors' use of air guns
A few states restrict minors' use of air guns, and such restrictions can apply to Paintball guns. For example, in New York, a person under 16 may not possess an air gun, or a firearm or ammunition, unless pursuant to a hunting permit. In California it is a criminal misdemeanour to sell air guns, including Paintball guns, to minors (under 18), and it is also a misdemeanour to furnish an air gun to a minor without the express or implied permission of the minor's parent or legal guardian. These restrictions have some effect on the game because minors, with parental permission, play Paintball in many states.

State toy gun laws A handful of states in addition to California have toy gun laws. These laws

▼ *A lookout for the opposition's attack team.*

may require toy guns to have special markings, make it a crime to brandish a toy gun so as to frighten another, punish one who commits a crime with a toy gun as if it had been committed with a firearm, or may prohibit the sale or manufacture of toy guns.

These laws are not being applied to Paintball guns. However, if a toy gun law is broadly worded, it could be misapplied to Paintguns. Where possible the IPPA has worked to clarify ambiguous laws. For example, in Connecticut a specific exemption for Paintball guns is written into the 1988 toy gun law.

State criminal laws for misuse of a Paintball gun In some states, commission of a crime with an instrument perceived to be a firearm (such as a toy gun or a Paintgun) is treated as seriously as if the crime were committed with an actual firearm. Similarly, in some states it is a crime to brandish an instrument perceived to be a firearm at another in a threatening manner. If a Paintgun were misused in these ways, criminal charges would be appropriate.

The IPPA is not aware of any laws that specifically refer to commission of a crime with a Paintball gun. However, there are instances where persons have committed crimes using Paintguns. For example, shooting street signs has resulted in vandalism charges in several states. Shooting a person with Paintballs while the person was walking on California city streets resulted in charges of battery. A man was arrested for felony child abuse in Wisconsin because he used his young children as moving targets, marking them with his Paintgun. All such criminal actions are abhorred by responsible Paintball players and the entire Paintball industry.

Players must remain aware of the fact that most members of the general public cannot distinguish a Paintball gun from a firearm and may be frightened if they see someone with a Paintball gun. If a citizen is sufficiently frightened or apprehensive, he or she may notify the police. In several states, players have carried Paintguns from their cars into a Paintball store or airsmith shop. Citizens seeing the Paintguns have called the police, saying they have seen someone with a 'firearm'. Such incidents create poor public relations for Paintball, and the IPPA recommends that, off the field, Paintguns be carried in bags or cases when carried in public view.

State law on sound suppressors Just as federal law makes possession of a silencer illegal without a permit, most states have their own comparable laws making possession of a firearm silencer illegal. Even a sound suppressor legal under federal law might not pass a given state's standards test and could be illegal within that state. Here again, one must consult local legal counsel to determine the legality of sales, possession, manufacture or permitting use of such devices in connection with a Paintball business.

Laws affecting more than one state Paintball guns and Paintball products are sold by mail throughout the USA. Since problems could arise, such as in connection with sales to minors in states where such sales are prohibited, those engaged in a mail order Paintball business should obtain legal advise regarding the laws of each state into which Paintball guns and Paintball products are sold. The IPPA is not aware of any criminal prosecutions that have arisen in connection with mail order sales of Paintball products.

Paintball guns may be taken on commercial airplanes if checked as charge baggage. Firearms must be declared and tagged under federal law, but since Paintguns are not firearms under federal law no such procedure is required. As a practical matter, however, it is suggested that a traveller tell airline personnel when checking baggage that a Paintgun is in the baggage. A Paintgun looks like a firearm to the baggage scanner, and if an airline believes there is a firearm in the bag, the bag may be detained until the passenger is contacted. There are no restrictions on taking your Paintgun from state to state, whether by plane or other means of transportation. Travel between countries depends on the laws of each country.

Local laws affecting Paintball In addition to federal and state laws, local laws may affect Paintball. One type of air gun law that affects Paintball is an anti-discharge ordinance. For example, the Los Angeles Municipal Code requires a police permit for discharge of an air gun in the city limits. Fields within the city limits must obtain a permit to operate.

Only one city, Chicago, attempting to deal with a high rate of juvenile crime, prohibits possession of Paintball guns within the city limits.

Players transporting their Paintguns from their homes in the city to fields outside the city have had Paintguns confiscated. No studies have ever correlated Paintball playing to criminal activity, in Chicago or elsewhere. The most significant local laws affecting

Paintball are zoning laws. These laws affect whether, where, and under what conditions indoor and outdoor Paintball fields can operate.

The IPPA has been involved in dozens of zoning cases, helping fields and stores open. The process by which you obtain a zoning permit usually requires an application and fee, inspections by regulatory agencies (fire department, building and safety, etc.), and public hearings both at or near the field site and before the zoning board. Most fields are able to obtain zoning approval to open. Those in very populated areas, without insurance, without good legal counsel and industry support throughout the proceedings, are most likely to fail.

All affected neighbours, landowners, tenants and businesses, receive notice of the public hearings. At the hearing before the zoning board, a testimony must describe the game and how it is played. Some legitimate concerns as to noise level, parking, sanitation and trash, safety of the games and non-toxicity of the Paintballs, use of referees and the like must be addressed.

An applicant must expect to respond to a group of persons who do not understand Paintball, have never played the game, and will protest the issuance of a permit. They will object to the image of the game as they understand it, of camouflage-clad, violence-prone, make-believe soldiers glorifying war, running through the woods playing army and shooting each other.

With testimony from players who are responsible members of the community and from industry leaders, and with good legal counsel, such protests can be overcome. Articles from Paintball magazines showing diversity of players, charity events and competitions, and accurately describing the game as 'Paintball' or capture the flag, should be presented. Documentation of the game's excellent safety record and its safety rules and equipment must be provided.

Favourable testimony will describe the extensive international scope of the sport, and its economic value to the community and the economy in general. Social benefits of the game are presented, as well as the fact that people from varied professions and of all nationalities and races play Paintball; nurses, doctors, police, firemen, secretaries, the hearing-impaired, actors, business owners and managers, lawyers, construction workers, students, and entire families. The absurdity of rejecting a game that is played and enjoyed by so many law-abiding adult citizens will emerge.

As pointed out in this section, many laws could apply to Paintball and some do affect it, but the game remains relatively regulation-free. Its safety record is excellent, and in a few short years Paintball has already made its mark.

Paintball in the 90s

The following information has been compiled by the International Paintball Players Association (the IPPA). The IPPA encourages growth of the sport of Paintball throughout the world.

How widespread is the sport of Paintball?

Paintball's public appeal is apparent from the phenomenal growth of the sport since the first game in 1981. There are approximately 500 identified Paintball facilities, outdoor and indoor, in the United States, and fields operate in all fifty states. American Sports Data Inc estimated that about 658,000 persons played Paintball in 1988, and the industry estimates that that figure is over a million players a year today. Paintball is played in about twenty-five countries world-wide. Canada estimates well over one hundred play sites, with a player base exceeding 100,000 players. The UK has an estimated 349 play sites. Paintball is spreading across Europe, throughout South and Central America and into the Far East.

Who plays the game of Paintball?

People of all ages, from all walks of life and all religions and nationalities play Paintball. Nurses, doctors, housewives, movie stars, secretaries, lawyers, stockbrokers, musicians, TV and radio personalities, the handicapped, construction workers, sales persons, artists and families enjoy the sport.

Paintball players work for minor and major companies alike and many businesses arrange Paintball outings for their companies, finding it not only recreational but also an activity that builds team spirit.

Church groups, scout troops and fraternities play Paintball. Law firms challenge their clients; rival insurance companies play matches. Wives play against husbands, girlfriends against boyfriends. Two chapters of the 'Millionaire Boys Clubs' have played a challenge match.

Paintball is played in the States on US Government lands by permit, and is played by government personnel. Paintball is played in the State of Arizona (Coronado National Forest) and the State of California, by US Government permit, on US National Forest Land.

The Hermitage Landing resort facility in Nashville, Tennessee, was the site for the 1988 NSG National Championships and the 1989 Line SI International Masters Tournament. Hermitage Landing is US Army Corps of Engineers' land. The United States Military Academy at West Point operates Paintball fields on government land at West Point. The Cadets have a three-year series of matches against the US Naval Academy, and West Point frequently hosts teams from surrounding states for special events and tournaments. In addition, the cadets have an ongoing extra-curricular Paintball program.

Recreational programs on military bases provide service personnel with recreational activity on, for example, Vandenberg Air Force, (CA) Fort Campbell (KY), Fort Knox (KY), Quantico Marine Base (VA) and Camp Pendleton Marine Base (CA).

Paintball has been used for training exercises by the US Navy on board various Naval ships, and by the US Army's 82nd Airborne. The 3rd Battalion of the 160th Infantry Regiment of the California Army National Guard played Paintball as part of a full battalion drill. Members of the California Army National Guard's 1st Battalion of the 185th Armored Regiment regularly played recreational

Paintball. The Texas Rangers have Paintball training exercises. The game is also recognized as a form of recreation played by personnel stationed on board US Navy ships.

In Oregon, a field operates by permit on state-owned land. Open government land is used for Paintball in various areas.

Who are the Paintball media?

Paintball's media include four internationally distributed US published magazines: *Action Pursuit* (CA), *Paintball* (CA), *Paintcheck* (NY) and *Paintball Sports* (NY). Two regional newspapers began publishing during the last six months in the USA. In the UK, *Paintball Games, Paintball Monthly* and *Paintball Adventures* are monthly magazines devoted to the sport. Numerous Paintball newsletters are also published throughout the world.

How does law enforcement utilize Paintball?

To help save officers' lives, law enforcement agencies use Paintball equipment in part of their programs, in both the USA and Canada. Indoor facilities are often used. For example, the Illinois Tactical Response Team, the Tennessee Correction Academy, the Sheriff's Department of Saginaw, Michigan and seven nearby Michigan departments all incorporate Paintball into their training programs. Many law enforcement officers world-wide enjoy playing the game for recreational purposes as well.

How do the law-makers look at Paintball?

In 1988, following discussion favourable in both the US Senate and House of Representatives, the US Congress recognized Paintball as a form of adult recreation as it exempted Paintball guns from the federal 'toy gun' marking law. In 1988, four state legislatures including California had bills pending that would have impacted adversely upon the sport of Paintball. Three were rewritten before passage, to protect the rights of Paintball players, and the fourth was dropped in committee. In 1989, Illinois passed legislation to classify Paintball guns separately from

the category of firearms and protect the rights of Paintball players and the industry. A 1990 Ontario, Canada bill that would have required expensive permits to import Paintguns was not passed.

What is Paintball's safety record?

Statistics for 1987 and 1988 show Paintball is safer than almost all other recreational activities. In 1988, insurance statistics show Paintball had 0.31 yearly injuries per 1,000 participants, while, for example, the US National Safety Council statistics show tennis had 1.09, golf 1.13, swimming 1.30, fishing 1.37, racquetball 2.53, snow skiing 3.44, baseball 27.67.

Eye protection is mandatory under the IPPS safety rules and the rules of all Paintball insurance companies; additional safety equipment and playing rules enforced by referees combine to maintain the game's excellent safety record, NAPRA referees may work in conjunction with IPPA within the IPPA's Safety Certification program, conducting field inspections. The North American Paintball Referees' Association (NAPRA) requires a training course, first aid and CPR certification for all its members. Paintball is played in more than twenty countries today and is particularly popular in the USA, Britain and Canada. Supporters from around the world have joined the IPPA and it is working to establish international standards of safety and competition.

For specific information about IPPA activities affecting your country please write to the IPPA International Co-ordinator: Donald E. de Kieffer, International Paintball Players Association, 864 Sconset Lane, McLean, Virginia 22102, USA.

Paintball in Belgium

To include in this book sites in Europe the Author sent out hundreds of leaflets, but as time was pressing due to the publication date, the response was rather limited.

In the Benelux areas of Europe there are various operators of sites, including one or two military sites. Mainly these sites are supplied with weaponry from the UK and sometimes directly from the USA.

Land use in Belgium is under intense pressure and where sites may be available, political forces, usually in the shape of the local mayor, can prevent a site being developed. In any case, where sites are

► *A double head shot demonstrates the value of goggles and helmet.*

allowed, strict land use rules apply, and must be enforced. The Paintball player must be aware of the very active Green Party, a political party that regards any land use other than natural as a serious environmental concern.

Having overcome these difficulties, which took eighteen months, Fireball Europe Ltd now believe that they have one of the larger European sites with more than fifty acres of woodland, sand dunes and lakes.

On site there are eight separate game areas and the varied terrain dictates the type of game scenario. Access to the site is easy, it being but a short drive from a nearby motorway. The location of the site is near Turnhout, roughly thirty miles from Eindhoven, Tilburg and Antwerp, and about fifty miles from Brussels and Ghent.

For full details contact Eric Hallam, Fireball Europe Ltd, Heilig Geestrstraat 7, B-2000 Antwerp, Belgium. Tel: 03/225 14 43.

◄ *Cannon with sight gives a good idea of the paint coverage of this weapon.*

▲ *A selection of typical Paintball weaponry.*

Organizers and equipment stockists

The following is a complete, world-wide directory of Paintball sites, equipment stockists and Paintball games organizers known at the time of publication.

ALABAMA (USA)
Freight Paintball Accessories, 1114 1/2 Jackson Highway, South Sheffield, AL 35660 205-381-3201.
Splat Alley Inc, 705 McKinley Ave, Huntsville, AL 35801 205-539-5959.
Advanced Alabama Adventures Inc, 7040 Bear Creek Road – 43 Sterrett, AL 35147 (205) 672-2860.
Alabama Paintball Supply, PO Box 180082, Mobile, AL 36618-0082 (205) 344-1757.
Paintball South Inc, 114 Corrine Drive, Madison, AL 35758 (205) 830-1319.
Possum-Trot Field, PO Box 268, Vincent, AL 35178 (205) 672-7753.
Pursuit South, 1814 First Avenue South, Pell City, AL 35125 (205) 388-7014.
Slaughter's Run Inc, 1014 5th Ave S.E., Decatur, AL 35601 (205) 350-5534.

ALASKA (USA)
United Survival Adventures, PO Box 189, Kasilof, AK 99610 (907) 262-2243.

ARIZONA (USA)
Southwest Airgun Recreation Co, 2647 Beverly Lane, Yuma, AZ 85365 602-726-6550.
Survival & Army Surplus, 15231 N. Cave Road, Phoenix, AZ 85032 602-482-6663.
Diamond In The Rough, Redington HCR, 890 Benson, AZ 85602 (602) 385-2300.
Diamond In The Rough, 329-B McNab Parkway, San Manuel, AZ 85631 (602) 385-2300.
Hualapai Mountain Combat Grounds, 2605 Hearne, Kingman, AZ 86401 (602) 757-1857.
Westworld Combat Games, 15231 N. Cave Creek Road, Phoenix, AZ 85032 (602) 482-6663.

ANGUS (SCOTLAND)
Survival Game (Angus), 0241 71363.

AUSTRALIA
Skirmish, PO Box 169, Olinda 3788 Victoria. 03-7512002.
Gold Coast War Museum, Springbrook Road, Mudgeeraba, Queensland. 075-305222.
S. Battalions Of Australia, 2 Cannon Court, Noble Park, North Melbourne, 3174.
Skirmish, PO Box 934, Unley 5061, Adelaide, South Australia. 08-3710776.
The Splat Shop, Skirmish Paintball, 23 McEachern Cres, Melba A.C.T. 2615, Canberra, Australia. 62-531-888.
Paintball Australia Pty, Box 444, Burleigh Heads 4220, Gold Coast. (075) 305222.

AVON (ENGLAND)
Combat Forest, Bath, 0225 336432/0225 316377.
Gunball Assault, Underground Game, Bath, 0373 65714 0373 84708.
Hamburger Hill, 0761 72611.
Mayhem Paintball Games Ltd, Marston (near Frome) 037384 325/497.
South-West Counties Paintball Supplies, Westfield Trading Estate, Unit D2, Westfield Nr Bath. 0761 412740 0860 290841.
Splat Attack, Bristol, 0272 604926.
Ultimate Game, 0272 604926.

AYRSHIRE (SCOTLAND) Challenger
Wargames, 0505 873587.
Camp Run-A-Muck, 0292 265756/284777.
Battlefield Wargames, 11 Lowther Bank, Irvine, Ayrshire, KA11 1EG, 0294 215975.

BELGIUM
Antwerp Paintball Company, Konijenberg 41, 2070-Antwerp, Belgium.
Fireball Europe Ltd, Heilig Geeststraat 7, B-2000, Antwerp, Belgium. Tel: 03/225 14 43.

BEDFORDSHIRE (ENGLAND)
Paintball Aventure Games, 0327 300641.
Skirmish, 0933 314805.
Survival (Leighton Buzzard), 0442 833314 0860 375055.
The Great Adventure Game, 0234 266266.
Survival (Old Warden), 0442 833314.

BERKSHIRE (ENGLAND)
Crossfire, 0753 27223.
Skirmish, 071-493 0270.
Platoon (Windsor site), 0753 580438.
Simulated Activities, 0734 345299.
Battle Group Wargames 'A', 0836 616992.
California Commando (Reading site), 0344 861099.
Battle Games UK Ltd (Amersham), 0923 897090.
Mayhem Paintball Games Ltd (Caversham Area), 0836 708625.
Professional Paintball, 06284 75909.

BORDERS (SCOTLAND)
Mayhem Paintball Games Ltd, Border Paintball Games Ltd (Nr Selkirk), 036 16411.

BUCKINGHAMSHIRE (ENGLAND)
The Wacky Adventure Team, Survival Game UK Ltd (High Wycombe), 0277 200488.
Army Games (UK) Ltd (Chesham site), 0702 232474, 0494 778465.
Termination (Milton Keynes), 0908 560529/ 669468.
Paintball Adventure Game (Milton Keynes), 0327 300641.
Battlegames UK (Amersham site), 0923 897090.
Blitz (Milton Keynes), 0908 320922.
Challenge (Amersham) BGF Affiliated, 0860 726228, 0923 819059.
Skirmish, 0933 314805.

CALIFORNIA (USA)
Aerostar West, 849 W Lambert Road, Unit B, Brea, CA 92621 (714) 529-7012.
Auction Surplus, 512 South Blosser Road, Santa Maria, CA 93454-4910 (805) 928-7405.
Adventure Game Supplies, 9641 Artesia Blvd, Bellflower, CA 90706 (213) 804-4764.

Adventure Game Supplies, 19249 Colima Road, Roland Heights, CA 90274 (818) 708-3384.
Adventure Game Supplies, 17618 Sherman Way, Van Nuys, CA 91405 (818) 708-3384.
Adventure Game Supplies, 1102 East Chestnut, Santa Ana, CA 92701 (714) 667-1166.
Auburn Army & Navy, 4535 Auburn Blvd, Sacramento, CA 95841 (916) 485-1120.
Boulder Battles, Pipes Canyon, CA 92268 (619) 228-1680.
Bakersfield Paintball Supply, 3523 Gilmore Ave, CA 93308 (800) 462-4359.
CA Supply Line, 15723 Vanowen St, Ste 109, Van Nuys, CA 91406 (818) 705-3630.
Cambrian Surplus, 2059 Woodland Rd, San Jose, CA 95124 (408) 377-6953.
California Paintball Supply, 421 El Cajon Blvd, El Cajon, CA 92020 (619) 440-5944.
Combat Arms, 2869 Grove Way, Castro Valley, CA 94546 (415) 538-6544.
Confederate Army Supplies, 9810 Owensmouth, Unit 8, Chatsworth, CA 91311 (818) 998-1862.
Delta Archery's Splat Division, 1820-D Arnold Ind. Way Concord, CA 94520 (415) 685-7141.
Field Patrol Games, PO Box 183, Oakley, CA 94561 (415) 625-4776.
Fields of Honor, 177 Cochran St-L Simi Valley, CA 93065 (805) 522-3939.
Fields of Honor (Chatsworth) 2034, Sycamore Dr, Simi Valley, CA 93065 (805) 5223939.
Fontana Paintball Supply, 16876 Foothill Blvd, Fontana, CA 92336 (714) 355-7707.
Foxhunters, 2568 San Carlos Ave, Castro Valley, CA 94546 (415) 582-Guns.
Gramps & Grizzly Paintball Guns, 7203 Arlington Ave, Unit F, Riverside, CA 92503 (714) 359-4859.
Golden West Supply Co, 1536 S. Myrtle Ave, Monrovia, CA 91016 (818) 357-0711.
Hawk Paintball Supply, 1924 West Mission Ave, Unit N, Escondido, CA 92025 (619) 745-2222.
Hobby World, 18575 Valley Blvd, Bloomington, CA 92316 (714) 877-3775.
The HQ Army Navy Store, 1735 Montebello Town Center, Montebello, CA 90640 (213) 727-9852.
The HQ Army Navy Store, 245 Carson Mall, Carson, CA 90746 (213) 532-1541.
Indoor Speedball, 15000 Avalon, Gardena, CA 90248 (213) 323-1021.
I&I Sports, 3840 Crenshaw Blvd, Suite 108, Los Angeles, CA 90008 (213) 715-6800.
Kingsman Shop, 201 North Hill St, Oceanside, CA 92054 (619) 722-5108.
Lion's Lair Paintball Park, 1036 Dos Rios Road, Laytonville, CA 95454 (707) 987-8057.

Long Beach Army Surplus, 7722 Garden Grove Blvd, Westminster, CA 92683 (714) 892-8306.
MC Paintball Supplies, PO Box 1383, Temecula, CA 92390 (714) 676-5416.
Nor-Cal Paintball Outlets, 2818 Foskett Avenue, Concord, CA 94520 (415) 872-8910.
North County Paintball Park, San Marcos, CA 92069 (619) 273-444.
The Outback, CA 15691 Laguna Ave, Elisnore, CA 92330 (714) 798-0527.
Outdoor World, 136 River Street, Santa Cruz, CA 95060 (408) 423-9555.
Paintball Connection, 7920 Miramar Road, Suite 123, San Diego, CA 92126 1-800-722-5594.
Paintball Hill, PO Box 41, Pope Valley, CA 94567 (707) 956-3023.
Paintball Paradise, 260 Shotwell Street, San Francisco, CA 94110 (415) 552-5335.
Hawk Paintball Pursuit, 4318 Case Street, San Diego, CA 92109 (619) 273-4444.
Paintball Mountain, 6751 N. Blackstone, Box 432, Fresno, CA 93710 (209) 228-1671.
Paintball Pro Shop, 8679 La Mesa Boulevard, La Mesa, CA 92041 (619) 469-1437.
Patton Field War Games, San Diego, CA (619) 299-6416.
Palmer Pursuit Shop, 11480 Sunrise Gold Circle, Unit B, Rancho, Gordova, CA 95742 (916) 631-8969.
Rene's Opposing Force, 7701 Melrose Avenue, Los Angeles, CA 90046 (213) 653-9126.
Ric's Adventure Games, 19289 Colima Road, Roland Heights, CA 90274 (818) 965-8038.
Sat Cong Village, 23441 Golden Springs, Ste. 243, Diamond Bar, CA 91765 (714) 620-6335.
Skan-Line, 1663 Superior Avenue, Unit B, Costa Mesa, CA 92627 (714) 645-5463.
Skirmish South Bay, 15630 Crenshaw Boulevard, Gardena, CA 90249 (213) 715-6670.
Skirmish Inc, 7117 Canby Avenue, Reseda, CA 91335 (818) 705-6322.
Spotcha Paintball Games, 828 North 2nd Street, El Cajon, CA 92021 (619) 444-7938.
Surplus City, 4106 Franklin Boulevard, Sacramento, CA 95820 (916) 485-1120.
Survival Sports, 4800 Minnesota Avenue, PO Box 661947, Fair Oaks, CA 95628 (918) 965-1770.
Taps, The Adventure Palace & Stadium, 661 Walsh Avenue, Santa Clara, CA 95050 (408) 748-1188.
Turner's Outdoorsman, 1214 West Francisquito Avenue, West Covina, CA 91790 (818) 917-8368.
Trader Sports Inc, 685 East 14th Street, San Leandro, CA 94577 (415) 569-0555.

Taskforce Survival Games Supplies, 1464 Graves Avenue, Suit 108, El Cajon, CA 92021 (619) 441-0491.
Unique Sporting/Strategic Game Supply, 10680 Katella Avenue, Anaheim, CA 92804 (714) 772-3583.
Valley Raceway, 9433 Valley Boulevard, Rosemead, CA 91770 (818) 443-0854.
Value Centre, 1121 East Colorado Boulevard, CA 91205 (818) 243-7265.
War Zone, 12500 Temescal Canyon Road, Corona, CA 91719.
War Zone, 10373 Powder River Court, Fountain Valley, CA 92708 (714) 963-1302.

COLORADO (USA)
Adventure Games of America Inc, PO Box 440776, Aurora, CO 80044 (303) 893-4263.
Aerostar of Colorado, Mile High War Games Supplies, 3215 Flower Street, Wheat Ridge, CO 80033 (303) 329-8349.
Paint Pellet Game, PO Box 5355, Arvada, CO 80005 (303) 469-3866.
The Paint Pellet Game, 9348 West 40th Drive, Westminster, CO 80021 (303) 469-3866.
Pro-Star Labs, RMT Sports, PO Box 1281, Littleton, CO 80160 (800) 423-4263.

CONNECTICUT (USA)
Paintball Arena, 290 South Frontage Road, New London, CT 06320 (203) 437-1575.
The Pistol Grip, 3467 Windsted Road, Torrington, CT 06790 (203) 489-9969.
Bill's Video, 124 South Main Street, Danielson, CT 06239 (203) 779-0140.

CHANNEL ISLANDS (UK)
Splattack Ltd (Fauxquets Valley Camp Site) 0481 714959.

CAROLINA (NORTH) (USA)
Adventure–UAA, 210 Ives Street, Havelock, NC 28532 (919) 447-5222.
Flying Colours Adventures Inc, PO Box 1677, Clemmons, NC 27012 (919) 788-4658.
Strategy Games of Charlotte Inc, 5540 Elisnore Place, Charlotte, NC 28212 (704) 532-9797.
Triangles Air Gun Games Ltd, 715 Pinewood Drive, Apex, NC 27502 (919) 362-4547.
Idol's Adventure Sport, Highway 74 West, Rockingham, NC 28379.

CAROLINA (SOUTH) (USA)
Combat USA, 429 Koon Store Road, Columbia, SC 29203 (803) 786-4539.
National Paintball Supply Company, 1200 Woodruff Road, Unit C-36, Greenville, SC 29607 (803) 458-7221.
Red Fox Games, 1 Red Fox Run, Woodruff, SC 29388 (803) 439-9484.
Opposing Forces, 4000 Leesburg, Hopkins, SC 29061 (803) 783-5725.

CARIBBEAN (PUERTO RICO)

Caribbean Water Craft, 1747 Central Avenue, Rio Piedras, PR 00920 (809) 793-8345.
Land of Oz Toy Store, Royal Dane Mall, St Thomas, VI 00802 (809) 776-7888.
Kings Jewellers, Munoz Riviera 105, Fajardo, PR 00648 (809) 863-0909.
Seven Seas Bike Shop, 53 Union, Fajardo, PR 00648 (809) 863-8981.
Caribe Liquor, 170 Calle Florida, Luquillo, PR 00673 (809) 889-6226.
TBT Inc, PO Box 1557, Luquillo, PR 00673 (809) 889-3685.

CANADA

Capture The Flag, Box 610, Cochrane, Alberta, TOL OWO (403) 932-3402.
Weekend Warriors, R.R.2, Olds, Alberta, TOM 1PO (403) 556-2132.
EAgle's Nest, 1691 North Island Highway, Campbell River, Vancouver Island, British Columbia V9W 2E6 (604) 286-9696.
NW Flag Adventures, 21165 117th Avenue, Maple Ridge, British Columbia V2X 2H1 (604) 463-9543.
SAS Paintball Games, 1045 Haslam Avenue, Victoria, British Columbia V9B 2N3 (604) 478-4725.
Canard Valley Paintball, R.R. 1 McGregor, Ontario, NOR 1JO (519) 726-5105.
Flagswipe Inc, 57 Dalhousie Crest, London, Ontario N6K 1N7 (519) 473-2524.
Forest City Paintball Supplies, 1082 Chippawa Drive, London, Ontario NSP 217 (519) 659-4354.
Four Seasons Games, 792 Marenette, Windsor, Ontario N9A 1Z6 (519) 971-0479.
The Great White Bear Hunt, Survival Game Inc, 100 Burrows Hall Boulevard, Unit 90, Scarborough, Ontario M1B 1M7 (416) 293-2023.
RLD Games Ltd, PO Box 209, 350 Brawley Road West, Brooklin, Ontario L0B 1C0 (416) 293-3903.
Ultimate Adventures, 76 Cardish Street, Klienburg, Ontario CD L0J (416) 259-1267.
Adventure Division, T & B Inc, 560 Shea, Boliel, Quebec J3G 3S8 (514) 441-1129.
Adventure Division Inc, 860 Bernard Pilon, McMasterville, Quebec CD J3G 5WA (514) 441-1129.
Badlands Inc, 3804-A Bloor Street, Etobicoke, Ontario CD M9B 6C2 (416) 698-4933.
Canadian Paintball Supplies Ltd, 6 Brucedale Avenue West, Hamilton, Ontario CD L9C 1C2 (416) 383-9614.
Combat Pursuit, 136 Martin Street, Milton, Ontario CD L8G (416) 878 3262.
Exotech Paintball Supply, 2 Walker Avenue, Stony Creek, Ontario CG L8G 1S6 (416) 643-0042.
Friendly Feud RR 2, Scotsburn, Nova Scotia CD BOK 1RO (902) 485 8463.
Flag Raiders, 667 Hamilton Street, Cambridge, Ontario N3H 3E3 (519) 653 3322.
Gotch Game, 69 West Burnside, Victoria, BC CD V9A 1B6 (604) 389 0717.
La Conquête du Drapeau, 1100 L'Achigan St East, New Glasgow, Quebec CD J0R 1J0 (514) 437 3171.
Les Equipements Survival Enr, 137 St Jacques Street, St Jean sur Richelieu, QC CD J3B 2K2 (514) 346 2709.
Northwest Flag Adventures, 3555 Pearkes Street, Port Coquitain, BC CD V3B 5E4 (604) 463 9545.
Pursuit Marketing Inc, 875 Foster Avenue, Suite 107, Windsor, Ont CD N8X 4W3 (519) 972 5440.
Pursuit Supplies International, 10243 84th St, Edmonton, Alberta CD T6A 3R1 (403) 466 5271.
Splat Shot, 6256 Quin Pool Road, Halifax N.S CD B3L 1A3 (902) 421 3211.
Survival Game, 69 West Burnside, Victoria B.C CD V9V 1B6 (604) 389 0717.
Quest for Adventure, 11319 57th Street, Edmonton, Alberta CD T5W 3V3 (403) 477 9252.
Rebel Manufacturing, RR 1 Delaware, Ontario CD LOL 1EO (519) 652 6092.
RDL Games Limited, PO Box 209, 350 Brawley Road, W. Brooklin, Ontario, CD LOB 1LC (416) 655 8955.
Superior Firepower, 25 Pol Ct, St Thomas, Ontario, Canada N5R 5P9 (519) 633 5390.

CAMBRIDGESHIRE (ENGLAND)

Outpost 90 (Huntington) 0480 812258 (Mobile), 0860 734153.
Saturday and Sunday Soldiers (Northampton) 0604 882278.
Mayhem Paintball Games Limited, Battle Group Wargames B, 0344 422055.
Action Attack Paintball Games (Bassingbourne), 0763 247815.
Mayhem Paintball Games (Peterborough), 0778 34177.

CHESHIRE (ENGLAND)

Simulated Activities, Frodsham, Cheshire 09282 2159.
Battle Action Zone, 0260 277746.
Shoot and Survive (SAS) Stalybridge, 0663 46961.
Skirmish, 051 336 6365.
Survival Game (Cheshire) , 0538 34232.

CORNWALL (ENGLAND)

Survival Game (UK) Limited, 0208 82226.
Tactical Assault, 0566 775543.

COUNTY DURHAM (ENGLAND)

Crossfire War Games (Bishop Auckland), 091 521 0089.
Mayhem Paintball Games Limited, Woodland Combat, 0325 353911.
Monument Paintball Adventures, 091 389 0901.
Skirmish, 0947 841423.

DELAWARE (USA)

Aerostar of Delaware, RD 3, Box 303A, Laurel, DE 19956 (302) 875 4544.

DAKOTA (NORTH) (USA)

Kamo Enterprises, 1212 1st West, West Fargo, ND 58078 3008 (701) 282 7315.
North Dakota Survival, 313 North 19th Street, Bismark ND 58501 (701) 224 8296.

DERBYSHIRE (ENGLAND)

Action Pursuit Centre (Tuxford, Nottinghamshire), 0777 871866.
Action Paintball (Buxton), 0298 22364.
Academy Wargames, 0332 864796.
Ambush Combat Game (Chesterfield), 0246 201001.
Havoc Wargames, 0889 502201.
Paintball Command, Central Bookings, 0924 252123.
WPL Paintball Games (BGF Affiliated Site), 0332 510761.

DORSET (ENGLAND)

Combat Zone (South), 0202 883024.
Dorset Paintball (Maiden Newton Site), 0202 623763.
The Great Escape (Blandford), 071 379 5798.
Ultimate challenge, 0202 861361.

DUMFRIES (SCOTLAND)

Skirmish, 038 782538.

DEVON (ENGLAND)

Skirmish (Plymouth site), 0752 342278.
Skirmish (Exeter), 0548 531661.
Survival Game (UK) Limited, Barnstaple Site 027 185 279.
Survival Game (UK) Limited, Exeter Site 0626 852268.
The Wargame Company, 0626 852366.
Warscape Devon Paintball, Kennford, Nr Exeter, 0392 833473.

EAST SUSSEX (ENGLAND)

Mayhem Paintball Games Limited, Paintball Raiders, 0452 306117.
Scalemead (Paintball guns and suppliers of balls, and game packs), 34 283 4433.
Skirmish, 0580 880 308.
Ambush Tactical Games, 0323 642321.
Battle Games UK Limited (Nutley), 0923 897090.
California Commando, Tunbridge Wells, 0580 713187.
Conflict Paintball Games (Hastings/Rye Area), 0424 441798.
Crossfire (Hove), 0273 732036.
Fireball, 0323 843878.
Splatt Sports, 0903 830905.
The Great Adventure Game, 0903 892890.

EAST YORKSHIRE (ENGLAND)
Garrison, 0964 670496.
Leeds Paintball Megastore, 0532 439797.

EDINBURGH (SCOTLAND)
Skirmish, 031 316 4004.
Bedlam Wargame Limited, 031 555 1945.
Mayhem Paintball Games Limited, 0506 880752.
Survival Game (UK) Limited, Livingstone, 0506 35235.
Survival Game (UK) Limited, Edinburgh, 031 554 4690.

ESSEX (ENGLAND)
Ambush Paintball Game (SE Essex) 0268 764553.
Apocalypse Now, 0702 471847.
Arena Warzone (Purfleet) 0708 865203.
California Commando (Colchester) 0206 222213.
Combat London Ltd, 081 502 3751.
Combat UK, 0268 413092.
Counter Attack, 0245 257721.
Coxy's Paintball International, 0375 644121.
Coxy's Paintball Consortium, 0702 73682.
Essex Battlefield (Brentwood) 04023 76879.
Essex Survival Adventure & Combat Centres, 0702 232474.
Fireball Adventures (UK) Ltd, (Snarl Ltd) 081 593 6543.
Fireball Essex, 0708 721580.
Mash Paintball Games Ltd 0708 32614.
Mash Paintball Games Ltd (Clacton/Weeley) 0255 430830.
Mayhem Paintball Games Ltd 0402 8517.
Operation Wolf (Harlow) 04027 50116.
Paintball Plus (Brentwood) 0277 234185.
Part-Time Heroes (Epping) 081 561 8993.
Phoenix Gun Co 0702 714872.
R&R Paintball (Romford) 0708 40387.
Skirmish 0708 723267.
Splat Attack 0245 350741.
West Point (Billericay) 0245 257721.
Tactical Air Pursuits (Basildon) 0268 683321.
The Predators War Games (Maldon) 0621 855460.
The Wacky Adventure Team, Survival Game UK Ltd (Ongar) 0277 200488.
The War Game Company (Colchester) 0206 764243.

FLORIDA (USA)
Hans Hobby Shop, 1202 W Waters Ave, Tampa, FL 33604 (813) 935-7782.
Korner Tradin' Post, 8300 49th Street, North, Pinellas Park, FL 34665 (813) 544-9253.
Mega-Elite, 10428 Acme Road, West Palm Beach, FL 33414 (407) 793-1351.
South Florida Tactical Pursuit, 2561 SW 92 Court, Miami, FL 33165 (305) 221-3833.
AFM Combat, 901 Cesery Boulevard, Jacksonville, FL 3221 (904) 743-7110.

American Combat Games, 5701 Park Boulevard, Pinelas Park, FL 34665 (813) 546-8096.
GT Gear Company, 7958 Pines Boulevard, Suite 225, Pembroke Pines, FL 33024 (305) 347-0429.
Guerrilla Games, 111 West Olympia Avenue, Punta Gorda, FL 33950 (813) 627-8865.
Headquarters Military Surplus, 1450 Skipper Road, Tampa, FL 33619 (813) 971-8805.
Holly Army Navy, 3440 Avenue, GNW Winter Haven, FL 33880 (813) 967-5920.
Island Adventure Combat Games, Snead Island, Tampa Bay Area-St Petersburg, FL 33711.
Mike's Guns & Paintball PX, 10428 Acme Road, West Palm Beach, FL 33406 (407) 439-0755.
Paintball Express, 11398 West Flager Street 202, Miami, FL 33174 (305) 221-0160.
Paintball World, 710 SW The Street, Suite 304, Miami, FL 33144 (305) 267-1122.
Paintball Pursuit Games Inc, 5148 Conroy Road, Suite 1238, Orlando, FL 32811 (407) 843-3456.
Sunny's at Sunset Inc, 8260 Sunset Strip, Sunrise, FL 33322 (305) 741-2070.
Survival City, 111 West Olympia Avenue, Punta Gorda, FL 33165 (813) 629-0909.
Topic Trades, 9696 SW 40th Street, Miami, FL 33165 (305) 221-1371.
Van's Military Surplus, 3598 Fowler Street, Fort Myers, FL 33901 (813) 939-1171.

GEORGIA (USA)
Adventure Game of Georgia-Marietta, 9401 Roberts Drive, NW 25-C, Dunwoody GA 30350 (404) 594-0912.
Arkem Stone Paintball, 7257 Cedar Crest Road, Acworth GA 30101 (404) 974-2535.
Atlanta Survival Game, 5720 Grove Point Road, Alpharetta GA 30201 (404) 623-0241.
Warpaint Games Ltd, 3292 Dug Gap Road, SW Dalton, GA 30720 (404) 694-8353.

GLASGOW (SCOTLAND)
Intercept 0563 17810.
Mayhem Paintball Games Ltd 041 425 1066.
Skirmish (North Glasgow) 031 316 4004.
Skirmish (South Glasgow) 038 782 538.
Strategy/Action Adventures 0501 32401.
Survival Game (UK) Ltd 041 638 2811.
Wargames Leisure 041 884 7403.

GLOUCESTER (ENGLAND)
Brentlands Battlefields 0453 872485.
Mayhem Paintball Games Ltd 04352 6189.
Mayhem Hereford (Forest of Dean Area) 0989 63783.

GRAMPIAN (SCOTLAND)
Skirmish (Aberdeen) 03308 414.

GREATER LONDON (ENGLAND)
Active Pursuit Combat Games 081 807 0583.
Campaign Paintball Game 081 672 7711.
Combat Zone (Hewitts) 0959 34271.
Combat Zone (London) Ltd 081 502 3751.
Electroworks 071 837 6419.
Fireball Adventure (UK) 081 692 1661.
Gamemaster Ltd 0895 825108.
Invicta Profield (Eynsford) 03224 30087.
Mayhem Paintball Games Ltd Empire Arms (Indoor Site) 081 523 2509.
Skirmish (East London) 0708 32367.
Skirmish (North London) 0933 314805.
Skirmish (South East London) 071 637 3810.
Skirmish (South London) 0883 724422.
Skirmish (South West London) 0784 458477.
Skirmish (West London) 071 493 0270.
Streatham Armoury 081 769 0671.
Survival Game (UK) Ltd 071 928 1733.
Tactical Air Games 081 312 1324.
Teamforce 081 898 3587.
The Gun Shop 081 854 4883.
The Wargame Company 081 968 6595.
Warpaint 081 645 9049.
Weekend Warriors 081 427 2707.

GREATER MANCHESTER (ENGLAND)
Bush Wacker 0606 888602.
Skirmish 0254 86719.
Skirmish 061 338 4449.
Survival Game (UK) Ltd 061 428 0070 (North Manchester).
Survival Game (UK) Ltd 0538 34232 (South Manchester).

GUAM
AJS Recreational Equipment, PO Box 803, Agana, Guam. 96910 (671) 477-7515.
Garland's Gear, PO Box 442, Agana, Guam. 96910 (671) 734-3275.

HAMPSHIRE (ENGLAND)
Ambush (Southampton) Mark Dunford 0489 896308.
Ambush (Southampton) Jim Conway 0836 762787.
Counteract Enterprises 0252 334036.
Encounters, Ian & Janet Horton 0794 390590.
Isle of Wight Paintball Games, 0983 883215.
Mayhem Paintball Games Ltd, Nouveau Adventure Games 0705 291318.
Combat (Wargames) (UK) 0703 265842.
Paintball Adventure Game Supplies (Andover) 0264 332337.
Platoon (Oakley Site) 0734 332116.
Skirmish 0256 83628.
Survival Game (UK) Ltd (Basingstoke site) 081 877 5199.
Target 0705 471007.
The Great Adventure Game 0428 713152.

HAWAII (USA)

Survive Hawaii Paint Gun Combat Games and Sales, 2956A Kaloaluiki Street, Honolulu, HI 96822.
Survival Game Hawaii Inc, PO Box 26378, Honolulu, HI (808) 988-3110.
Tactical Airgun Games/Supply of Hawaii, 2118 Haena Drive, Honolulu, HI 96822 (808) 946-4441.

HEREFORD & WORCESTER (ENGLAND)

Mayhem Hereford 0989 64716.
Independent Paintball Games 0206 42884.
Skirmish 0905 426313.

HERTFORDSHIRE (ENGLAND)

Action Pursuit Centre 0923 897090.
Battles Games UK Ltd (Hook Wood) 0707 874438.
Battle Games UK Ltd (Pelum) 0707 874438.
California Commando (Hemel Hempstead) 09278 4944.
Challenger Tactical Sports Games S. Cockren, PO Box 407, Marsworth, Tring, Herts.
Combat Adventure 0279 730186.
Combat Adventure Game UK (Hoddesdon) 0992 589902.
Fireball Adventure (UK) Ltd, Active Combat Pursuit 081 884 2795.
Fireball Adventure Games (UK) Ltd, Combat Arena 0992 589902.
The Rogue Warrior (Hatfield) 081 427 0296.
Skirmish 0933 314805.
Sudden Impact 0442 890051.
Survival Game (UK) Ltd (Hatfield site) 071 928 1733.
The Wargame Company 081 968 6595.

HOLLAND

The Club Gotcha, Patrick's Paintball Place, Hoefblad 12, 1911 P,A UITGEEST, Holland.
Tel: 010 31 2513-14870.

HUMBERSIDE (ENGLAND)

Action Pursuit Centre (Tuxford Notts) 0777 971 866.
Garrison 0964 670496.
Survival Game (UK) Ltd 0472 240294.

IDAHO (USA)

The Clubhouse, 393 Park Avenue, Idaho Falls, ID 83402 (208) 523-5117.

ILLINOIS (USA)

Air Gun Designs, 301 Industrial Lane, Wheeling, IL 60090 (312) 520-7507.
A & M Sales Inc, 23 West North Avenue, Northlake, IL 60164 (312) 562-8190.
American Paintball Supply, 5607 West 79th Street, Burbank, IL 60459 (312) 422-8017.
American Wargames of Alsip, 14001 S.

Western Lot 180, Blue Island, IL 60406 (312) 371-0052.
Direct Connect Inc, 1131 W. 175th Street, Homewood, IL 60430 (312) 957-5858.
Emerald Forest Outdoor Games, 9200 S. 83 Avenue, Hickory Hill, IL 60457 (312) 430-3365.
Paintball Blitz, 2200 W. Higgens Road, 305 Hoffman Estates, IL 60195 (312) 882-0188.
Whiten Pantry, 7. S. 042 Main Street, Downers Grove, IL 60516 (312) 842-4705.
William's Combat Games Inc, PO Box 2171, Darien, IL 60559 (312) 963-7735.
Aerostar, 1416 S. Western Avenue, Posen, IL 60466 (708) 389-1300.
Ballmeisters, 201 North State Street, Chicago Heights, IL 50411 (708) 757-3333.
Blast Camp, 1927 West Hunbolt Boulevard Chicago, IL 60647.
JAS Military Supply, 1301 N. Broadway, Joliet, IL 60435 (800) 728-2769.
JAS/Normal Military Surplus, 1203 South Main Street, Normal, IL 61761.
Line of Fire, 1605 West 1st Avenue, Route 6, Coal Valley, IL 61240 (309) 799-5200.
MACS, 103 So. Third Street, Bellville, IL 62220 (618) 476-1323.
Master of the Game, 914 Greenwood Avenue, Glenview, IL 60025 (312) 988-8277.
Paintballers Inc, 201 No State Street, Chicago Heights, IL 60411 (708) 757-3333.
The Adventure Game, 3 South 571 Winfield Road, Warrenville, IL 60555 (708) 393-3637.
The Stealth Games, PO Box 13, Cordova, IL 61242 (309) 523-3898.

INDIANA (USA)

Adventure Game of Indianapolis, 1925 North Campbell Avenue, Indianapolis, IN 46218 (317) 356-5111.
Combat Connection, 5711 Calumet Avenue, Hammond, IN 46320 (219) 931-1122.
KEA Combat Games, RR 26, Box 353, Terre Haute, IN 47802 (812) 898-2766.
Emerald Forrest Outdoor Games, 925 East Millcreek, IN 47421 (812) 236-5800.
Stevens East Side, Rt 13 Highway 50 East, Bedford, IN 47421 (812) 279-9929.
Strategy Games, PO Box 2046, West Lafayette, IN 47906 (317) 463-5029.

IOWA (USA)

Adult Tactical Air Gun Games, RR 3, Keokuk, IA 52632 (319) 372-3849.
B&G Paintball Inc, PO Box 172, Mitchelville, IA 50169 (515) 967-6681.
Iowa Sport Combat/Game & Supply, PO Box 411, North Liberty, IA 52317 (319) 626-3148.
RIP Supply, 3615 North Broadway, Council Bluffs, IA 51503 (712) 322-7609.

IRELAND, REPUBLIC OF

Skirmish, Dublin 0001 933 043.

KANSAS (USA)

Splatoon Paintball Club, Box 339, Hugoton, KS 67951 (316) 544-2106.
Tactical Games Inc, 5A8 2401 West 25th Street, Lawrence, KS 66047 (913) 841-1884.
Adventure One Inc, 915 East 52nd Street South, Wichita, KS 67216 (316) 524-5557.
Lone Wolfe Paintball Games, 2707 South 38th Street, Kansas City, KS 66106 (913) 262-3748.
Lone Wolfe Paintball Supplies, 2707 South 38th Street, Kansas City, KS 66106 (913) 626-3748.

KENT (ENGLAND)

Action Tean 0424 51320.
Battle Zone 0634 725192.
Recon 0634 686756.
Battle Zone (Ron Barton) 081 303 0417.
California Commando UK Ltd, Head Office 0580 713187.
California Commando, Maidstone Site 0622 858501.
Challenge Paintball Ltd (Tunbridge Wells) 081 855 4487.
Combat UK (Doddington) 0268 413092.
Combat 311 (Maidstone) 0732 841741.
Coxy's Paintball International (Trade Warehouse) 0634 714768.
Fire-Fight (Nr Folkestone) 030389 2341.
Firepower Wargames (Kent) 0304 215761.
Fireball Adventure (UK) Ltd (Southfleet Site) 081 692 1661.
Frontline Wargames Ltd 0227 87560.
Intrepid Combat 0634 241560.
Invicta Profield (North Kent) 03224 30087.
Kent Survival (Canterbury) 0303 874282.
Mayhem Paintball Games Ltd 081 303 0798.
Mayhem Paintball Games Ltd (Marshlands) 0679 21466.
Mayhem Paintball Games Ltd (Canterbury) 0227 87560.
Medway 311 Paintball Shop 0634 724707.
Move Quick Ltd (Sidcup) 081 308 0709.
Paintball Heroes 081 367 4414.
Paintball Jungle (Ashford) 081 316 1037.
Skirmish (Wrotham) 071 637 3810.
Survival Game (UK) Ltd (Sidcup site) 071 928 1733.
Survival Game (UK) Ltd (Canterbury) 0634 864173.
Tactical Air Games Ltd (The A-Shau Valley) 03224 40316.
Tactical Air Games (The Store) 081 312 1324.
The Wacky Adventure Team (Tunbridge Wells) 0277 200488.

KENTUCKY (USA)

Blast, 3406 Greentree Road, Lexington, KY 40517 (606) 271-4599.

The Hit, 399 Pleasant Street, Covington, KY 41011 (606) 261-4031.

Eagle Army Navy/Combat Encounters, 1609 Bardstown Road, Louisville, KY 42445 (502) 458-ARMY.

Fox Hole, 500 Maple Avenue, Princetown, KY 42445 (502) 365-9655.

The Gunnery, 132 North Maine Street, Greenville, KY 42345 (502) 338-4010.

LANCASHIRE (ENGLAND)
Combat Quest (Burnley) 0282 36949.
Skirmish 0254 86719.

LEICESTERSHIRE (ENGLAND)
The Paint Connection (Nr Ashby-de-la-Zouch) 0530 70792.
Battlecamp 0536 61130.
Saturday & Sunday Soldiers (Northampton) 0604 882278.
Splatgun World 0530 510086.
Academy Wargames 0332 864796.

LINCOLNSHIRE (ENGLAND)
Action Pursuits Centre (Tuxford) 0777 871866.
Survival Game (UK) Ltd 0658 864421.

LOUISIANA (USA)
Flag Raiders, PO Box 640536, Kenner, LA 70064.
Flag Raiders, 17851 Million Dollar Road, Covington, LA 70433 (504) 893-7980.

MAINE (USA)
I & I Pursuit Games Inc, Abbot Road, Winslow, ME 04962 (207) 873 1953.
Woodland Warriors, PO Box 130, E Lebanon, ME 04027 (207) 457 1224.
Ramball, 9 Highland Avenue, Skowhegan, ME 04976 (207) 474 2838.
Van Houten Army/Navy Store, Lower Cross Road, PO Box 130, E Lebanon, ME 04027.

MARYLAND (USA)
Action Game Supply Inc, 3224 Maiden Lane, PO Box 833, Manchester, MD 21102 (301) 239 6702.
Battle Zone Inc, 550 N Craine Hwy 31, Glenburnie, MD 21061 (301) 760 8688.
Front Line Action Games, 14 E Jarrettsville Road, Forest Hill, MD 21050 (301) 879 7154.
MD Survival Games, PO Box 712, Seabrook, MD 20706 (301) 577 6111.
On Target Inc, 2618 Annapolis Road, Severn, MD 21144 (301) 551 7777.
Sportsman's Service Centre, Route 50, Chester, MD 21619 (301) 643 4545.
Standard Supplies, 14 Chestnut Street, Gaithersburg, MD 20877 (301) 464 1694.

MASSACHUSETTS (USA)
Adventure Game of America, PO Box 1054, E Arlington, MA 02174 (617) 391 5969.

Eastern Crossfire, Serving the Springfield/Worcester Area (413) 783 7999.
Eastern Massachusetts Paintball Games, 131 Ruby Road, Dracut, MA 01826 (508) 689 9553.
Ultimate Sports Inc, 45 Emerson Street, Brockton, MA 02401 (508) 559 0777.
Weekend Warrior, 6 Ellwell Street, Glouchester, MA 01930 (508) 283 1265.

MERSEYSIDE (ENGLAND)
Paintball Zone 051 733 4430.

MICHIGAN (USA)
Allen Park Paintball Supply, 6631 Allen Road, Allen Park, MI 48101 (313) 388 5111.
Direct Hit 22100 Coolidge Street, Ste 15, Oak Park, MI 48237 (313) 544 8635.
Hell Survivors Inc, 545 East Main Street, D 19, Bickney, MI 48169 (313) 878 5656.
Harry's Army Surplus, 201 E Washington Street, Ann Arbor, MI 48104.
Harry's Army Surplus Inc, 2050 N Telegraph road, Dearborn, MI 48128 (313) 565 6605.
Splatball City, PO Box 02147, Detroit, MI 48202 (313) 875 7549.
Splat Ball Survival Games, PO Box 5385, Saginaw, MI 48603 (517) 799 7633.
Splatz Limited, 7124 Cooley Lake Road, Union Lake, MI 48180 (313) 363 2500.
The Outpost A Combat Store, 26010 Eurek Road, Taylor, MI 48180 (313) 946 6451.
Young Army/Navy Surplus, 3416 S Westnedge Avenue, Kalamazoo, MI 49001 (616) 382 1900.

MINNESOTA (USA)
Paintball Express Inc, 20646 Jaguar Avenue, Lakesville, MN 55044 (612) 469 1888.
Splatball Inc, 1627 Washington Street NE, Minneapolis, MN 55413 (612) 788 6392.
Splat Zone Survival Inc, RR1, Box 270, Makato, MN 56001 (507) 278 4120.

MISSISSIPPI (USA)
Strategic Woodland Assault Tactics Inc, 1939 Pass Road, Biloxi, MS 39531 (601) 385 2264.

MONTANA (USA)
Blastmaster, RR1 Box 22A, New Franklin, MO 65274 (816) 848 2831.
Ground Zero, 255 Wolfner Dr, Fenton, MO 63026 (314) 487 6052.

NORWAY
Paintball Adventures Norway, Toyengaten 31, 0578 Oslo 5, Norway 011 47 2 198 440.

NEVADA (USA)
The Gun Trader, 1105 S Wells, Reno, NV 89502 (702) 786 4447.
Las Vegas Combat Fields, 4000 Boulder

Hwy, Las Vegas, NV 89121 (702) 387 1640.
Survival Store (Indoor Paintball) 2448 Losee Road, N Las Vegas, NV 89030.

NEW HAMPSHIRE (USA)
Pollard Associates/New England Paintball, 10 2nd Street, Dover, NH 03820 (603 742 1636).
Adventure Game of New Hampshire, 158 Deering Road, Weare, NH 03281 (603) 529 3524.
Beaulia's Army Navy, 24 Canal Street, Laconia, NH 03246 (603) 524 1018.
Bow Valley Supply, 7 River Road, Bow, NH 03301 (603) 224 0163.
Canobie Paintball, 47 Roulston Road, Windham, NH 03087 (603) 893 1863.
Combat Simulations, RFD 4, Box 425, Weare, NH 03821 (603) 592 FLAG.
Northeast Survival Supply, Rt 38, Box 654, Pelham, NH 03076 (603) 635 9049.
Seacoast Paintball Games, PO Box 173, Epping, NH 03042, 1 800 726 GAME.

NEW JERSEY (USA)
FG Woods Paintball Field and Supplies, 513 King's Hwy, Mickleton, NJ 08056 (609) 423 3936.
DLA Paintball Supplies, 28 Edwards Court, Bayonne, NJ 07002 (201) 436 9853.
MAZE, 89 Leuning Street, South Hackensack, NJ (201) 343 1277.
Performance Paintball, 7 Fifth Street, New Brunswick, NJ 0891 (201) 846 6427.
Pursuit Paintball Association, PO Box 185, Fort Murray, NJ 11795 (201) 689 2084.
Scorpions Den, 33 Third Street, Butler, NJ 07405 (201) 492 9036.
South Jersey Paintball Game, 1939 Rt 70 East, Suite 250, Cherry Hill, NJ 08003 (609) 772 2878.
South Jersey Paintball Supplies, 670 Route 45, Mantua, NJ 08051 (609) 468 6939.

NEW YORK (USA)
Forest Strategy Game Company, Knickerbocker Road, Schaghticke, NY 12154 (518) 664 5951.
Ho/Rc Hobbie, Ho 982 Monroe Avenue, Rochester, NY 14620 (716) 244 8321.
Hunt, Fish and Shoot, 291 West Main Street, Smithtown, NY 11787 (516) 979 8278.
JT's Paintball Zone Inc, Camp A-158, Altay Road, Rock Stream, NY 14878 (607) 535 7285.
Mad Mac's, 47 South Lake Boulevard, Mahopac, NY 10541 (914) 628 3488.
Mid Hudson Army/Navy, Rt 4, Wappinger Falls, NY 12590 (914) 297 0679.
Paintball Maniacs, 8516 17th Avenue, Brooklyn, NY 11214 (718) 331 5973.
Recreation North, 24 South Platt Street, Plattsburgh, NY 12901 (518) 561 8648.

Rex Army-Navy Paintball Supplies, 8601 18th Avenue, Brooklyn, NY 11214 (718) 236 1900.

Aerostar East, Rochester, NY 14616 (716) 865 2400.

Army Navy Surplus, 1158 George urban Boulevard, Cheektowaga, NY 14225 (716) 684 8728.

Assault Hill 1700, 1700 Minsteed Road, Newark, NY 14513 (315) 331 4980.

Bell Army and Navy, 40-48 Bell Boulevard, Bayside, NY 11361 (718) 224 5098.

Bell Army and Navy, 46 West Montauk Highway, Lindenhurst, NY 11757 (516) 957 4363.

Cousins Army and Navy, 19 Udall Road, West Islip, NY 11795 (516) 661 7419.

Precision Paintball, 2079A W.6th Street, Brooklyn, NY 11223.

Paintball Adventure, 10865 Wilson Road, Wolcott, NY 14590 (315) 587 4995.

Paintball Game Supply Inc, 160 Dispatch Drive, East Rochester, NY 14445 (716) 383 5662.

Paintball Madness, 8611 23rd Avenue, Brooklyn, NY 11214 (718) 714 4193.

Recon Challenge, 390 Columbia Turnpike, Rensselaer, NY 12144 (518) 477 7156.

Sacandaga Survival Game, Rural Delivery 1, Fishouse Road, Galway, NY 12074 (518) 882 6845.

Survival New York, 295 Main Street, Mt Kisco, NY 10549 (800) 87 SURVIVE.

NEW ZEALAND
Pursuit Marketing NZ Limited, 5 Nutfield Lane, Christchurch 2, New Zealand 03 327187.

Pursuit Marketing NZ, 46 Tiri Tiri Road, Birkdale, Auckland, New Zealand 09 436573.

NORFOLK (ENGLAND)
Renegade Games Park (Nr Diss) 0379 853117.

Skirmish 0603 610300.

The Great Adventure Game (Norfolk) 0692 406275.

Warzone (Kings Lynn) 0760 721852.

NORTHAMPTONSHIRE (ENGLAND)
Battlecamp (Corby) 0536 61130.

Frontline (Northampton) 0604 706856.

Pegasus Outdoor Pursuits (Kettering/ Wellingborough) 0536 522564.

Skirmish 0933 314805.

Splatchek Shop 0869 810008.

The Paintball Adventure Game 0327 300641.

Weekend Warriors (Bicester) 0734 760046.

NORTHUMBERLAND (ENGLAND)
Fireball Adventures (UK) Limited, Fireball Combat 0670 819400.

Ridge 175, Reivers of Tarset (North Tyne Valley) 0434 240245.

NORTH YORKSHIRE (ENGLAND)
Fireball Adventures (UK) Limited, Top Gun 0274 684415.

Leeds Paintball, Megastore 0532 439797.

Skirmish 0947 841432.

Transcan Paintball (York) 0831 494000.

Atax-Tix 0423 854887.

Woodland Combat Club 0325 721749.

NOTTINGHAM (ENGLAND)
Academy Wargames 0332 864796.

Action Pursuits Centre (Tuxford, Notts) 0777 871866.

Elite Paintball Adventures (Nottingham) 0602 474411.

Fireball Adventures (Notts) 0623 794155.

Mayhem Paintball Games Limited, Tack-Tics 0860 840764.

Skirmish 0602 410454.

Ultimate Survival 0836 693657.

OHIO (USA)
Action Enterprises, 1014 Raab Road, Swanton, OH 43558 (419) 826 0744.

Battlefield War Games, 3825 April Lane, Columbus, OH 43227 (614) 236 4115.

BRAG, 3509 Vannest Avenue, Middletown, OH 45042 (513) 423 4858.

Combat Zone of America, 7060 S.TWP Road, 131 Tiffin, OH 44883 (419) 447 8424.

Cam-Sport Enterprises, 100 So Edgehill Drive, Fredericktown, OH 43019 (614) 694 1291.

Crossfire, 5318 State Road, Parma, OH 44134 (216) 351 1581.

Dano's Paintball, 1136 Richey Road, Felicity, OH 45120 (513) 876 2787.

Friendly Fire, 634 Reigert Square, Fairfield, OH 45014 (513) 896 6050.

Miami Valley Shooting Grounds, 7771 S Cassel Road, Vandalia, OH 45377 (513) 890 1291.

Mohican Outdoor Adventure Inc, PO Box 358, Loudinville, OH 44842 (614) 464 7024.

Northeast Survival, 4197 Pearl Road, Cleveland, OH 44109 (216) 749 2868.

Paintball Heaven, 2311 Argyle Street, Dayton, OH 45420 (513) 253 3599.

Pinnacle Woods Survival Game, 8752 East Avenue, Mentor, OH 44060 (216) 286 6167.

Seek and Exist, 3690 Halls Creek Road, Morrow, OH 45152 (513) 899 2954.

Staaf, PO Box 108, Robertsville, OH 44670 (216) 868 5225.

Strike Force, 1229 22nd NW, Canton, OH 44709.

Tusco Paintball Game, Route 4 Box 4389, Sunset Lane, New Philadelphia, OH 44663 (216) 339 4599.

Battlefield War Games, 7110 East Livingstone Avenue, Reynoldsburg, OH 43068 (614) 759 9219.

RW Ammo and Guns Paintball Equipment, 2311 Argyle, Dayton, OH 45420 (513) 253 3599.

Strike Force Akron-Canton, PO Box 317, Middlebranch, OH 44652 (216) 497 3898.

Strike Forest, 1801 Allen Road, Salem, OH 44460.

Willie's Paintball Games, 855 St Mary's Avenue, Sidney, OH 45365 (513) 492 9504.

OKLAHOMA (USA)
Sam's Off Road and Paintball, 4725 South Memorial, Tulsa, OK 74145 (800) 633 6716.

Slaughter's Venture, 4917 Northwest Pollard Avenue, Lawton, OK 73505 (405) 353 5178.

Sport Paint, 1916 South Gary Place, Tulsa, OK 74104 (918) 663 GAME.

OREGON (USA)
NY Sports and Games, 12705 SW Pacific Highway, Tigard, OR 97223 (503) 620 1141.

Apache Warpaint, 448 North Highway 99W, McMinnville, OR 97128 (503) 472 0921.

Splat Action Northwest, 23875 NE Dillon Road, Newberg, OR 97132 (503) 538 7305.

Splatman Supply, 1157 Cottage Street NE, Salem, OR 97301 (503) 370 7740.

Whack'm and Splak'm Paintball Adventures, PO Box 58, Keno, OR 97627 (503) 884 8942.

OXFORDSHIRE (ENGLAND)
Platoon (Ipsden Site) 0734 332116.

Survival Game (UK) Limited (Faringdon Site) 0367 20555.

Weekend Warriors (Bicester) 0734 760046.

Weekend Warriors 0734 761438.

PENNSYLVANIA (USA)
The Encounter, 515 Main Street, Stroudsburg, PA 18360 (717) 424 6132.

Main Line Survival Game, PO Box 101, Southeastern, PA 19399 (215) 630 6767.

Sgt York's Army-Navy Paintball Supply Store and Friendly 'Wargames', 900 Market Street, Lemoyne, PA 17043 (717) 761 3819.

Three Rivers Survival Games, 251 West View Road, Wexford, PA 15090 (412) 935 6100.

Cobra Command Inc, 41 Windsor Ct, Lausdale, PA 19446 (215) 855 7398.

Frontline 4369 Sunset Pike, Chambersburg, PA 17201 (717) 263 3700.

Kuba's Surplus Sales, 231 W 7th Street, Allentown, PA 18102 (215) 433 3877.

Roman's Army Store, 4369 Sunset Pike, Chambersburg, PA 17011 (717) 761 3819.

RHODE ISLAND (USA)

John's Army Surplus, Airport Plaza, 1800 Poast Road, Warwick, RI 02886 (401) 738 8735.

Rhode Island Survival Game Store, 1450 Hartford Avenue, Johnston, RI 02919 (401) 274 5118.

Scorpions Survival Game of Warwick, 492 Warwick Avenue, RI 02888 (401) 0099.

SHROPSHIRE (ENGLAND)

Salop Paintball Games 0952 502770.

SOMERSET (ENGLAND)

Hamburger Hill 0761 72611.

Mayhem Paintball Games Limited (Mayhem at Marston) 037384 325/497.

SOUTH AFRICA

Protectstick Manufacturers, PO Box 38192, 2016 Republic of South Africa.

SOUTH DAKOTA (USA)

Big Jim's Feud Ranch, HRC 30, Box 17, Spearfish, SD 57783 (605) 578 1808.

SOUTH YORKSHIRE (ENGLAND)

Woodland Games (Sheffield) 0226 207285.

Mayhem Paintball Games Limited, Ambush 0742 373417.

Paintball Commando 0924 252123.

Splatoon 0924 254339.

Survival Game (South Yorkshire) 0538 34232.

STAFFORDSHIRE (ENGLAND)

Action Paintball (Buxton) 0298 22364.

Havoc Paintball Games 0889 502201.

Skirmish 0785 660646.

Skirmish (South Staffs) 0902 758682.

Strikeout Adventure Games (Newcastle-under-Lyme) 0625 24979.

SUFFOLK (ENGLAND)

Bury Blitz IPG (Bury St Edmunds) 0284 810973.

California Commando (Ipswich Site) 0728 747474.

Mayhem Paintball Games Limited 0394 460475.

Skirmish 04493 672.

SURREY (ENGLAND)

Paintball Adventure Games (Cobham) 0753 855620.

Action Pursuit Limited (Lightwater) 0276 76676.

Campaign Paintball Games 081 6727711.

Contact Tactical Games 071 794 9269.

Fighting Force International (West Horsley) 081 942 2382.

The Great Adventure Game 081 878 9130.

Mercenary War Games (East Grinstead/Crawley) 0273 553919.

Paintball Sport Limited (Ottershaw) 0483 750296.

Mission Impossible/Thunderdome 0276 855456.

Predator Games (UK) (Croydon) 081 686 2228.

Skirmish 0883 723422.

Survival Game (UK) Limited (Leatherhead/Cobham Site) 0836 244463.

The War Game (nr Dunsford) 0784 51444.

The War Game Company 081 968 6595.

Top Gun Paintball Adventure Games (Guildford) 042 8795191.

TENNESSEE (USA)

Nashville Survival Games Inc, 536 W Hillwood Boulevard, Nashville, TN 37205 (615) 356 0213.

East Tennessee Survival Game, 4804 Ashville Highway, Knoxville, TN 37914 (615) 525 6831.

Games Unlimited Inc, 420 East Main Street, Gallatin, TN 37066 (615) 425 GAME.

Games Unlimited of Clarksville, Tinytown Road, Clarksville, TN 37042 (615) 647 4435.

Splatterball Adventure Games, 8813 Saint John's Road, Chattanooga, TN 37343 (615) 842 2340.

The War Zone Command, PO Box 16459, Memphis, TN 38186 (901) 785 5000.

TEXAS (USA)

Parinoid Park, Mauriceville, TX (409) 983 5007.

The Book Stand, 4805 Gulfway, Port Arthur, TX 77642 (409) 983 5007.

Ambush Valley Paintball Games, Area 290/1960, Houston, TX :713) 328 4561.

Direct Hit, 17017 Rolling Creek, Houston, TX 77090 (713) 440 3006.

Flag Quest, 2821 West Morton Street, Denison, TX 75020 (214) 463 1900.

Hunters Headquarters, 2200 Airport Freeway, Suite 480, Bedford, TX 76022 (817) 283 9100.

Lone Star Combat Games, 2513 West Ohio, Midland, TX 79701 (915) 694 1501.

TYNE AND WEAR (ENGLAND)

Soldier Field (Tyneside) 091 4107331.

Combat (Tyneside) 091 268 1500.

Crossfire War Games (Bishop Auckland) 091 5210089.

Monument Paintball Adventures 091 389 0901.

Strike Force (NE) 091 456 7632.

UTAH (USA)

Commando Games of Utah, 4352 West Draper Street, Kearns, UT 84118.

CCS/Air Assault, 175 East 400 Street, Suite 1000, Salt Lake City, UT 84111 (801) 350 9102.

Richards Hobbies and Sports, 4095 Riverdale Road, Ogden, UT 84405 (801) 394 9015.

PT Enterprises, 750 South 650 W.67, Provo, Utah 84601 (801) 377 6573.

Sure Shot Paintball Game, 1258 North Monroe, Ogden, UT 84404 (801) 782 7437.

VERMONT (USA)

Fox Hole, 35 North Main Street, White River Junction, VT 05001 (802) 295 7730.

Green Mountaineers Limited, 34 Forest Place, Brattleboro, VT 05301 (802) 254 6799.

VIRGINIA (USA)

Fredericksburg Military Surplus, 921 Caroline Street, Fredericksburg, VA 22401 (703) 371 7932.

The Gun Works, Rte 501, PO Box 613, Rustburg, VA 24588 (804) 332 5423.

Hobby town of Virginia, 1218 Blue Ridge Avenue, Culpeper, VA 22701 (703) 825 6729.

Lyons Trading Company, 4937 Americana Drive, 201 Annadale, VA 22003 (703) 642 5777.

Operation Base Hit, 804 Newtown Road, Building 102, Virginia Beach, VA 23464 (804) 473 9952.

Tech-Na-Ball Inc, 8202 MacBeth Street, Manassas, VA, 22110 (703) 335 5466.

The Ultimate Adventure Game, Route 653, Leesburg, VA 22075 (301) 464 1694.

The National Gun Sport Corporation, PO Drawer 290, Arc, VA 23003 (804) 693 5024.

Virginia Adventure Games Inc, PO Box 1778, Springfield, VA 22151 (703) 631 0909.

WALES (UK)

Paintball Platoon Games, Rhyl, North Wales 0745 570 082.

Questors Leisure 0222 493334.

Surviva (Llandeilo) 0442 833314.

Paintball Combat (Mid Glamorgan) 0656 772095.

Skirmish 051 336 6365.

Splatball Limited (Cardiff & Newport) 0564 32537.

Adventure Sports Leisure (Mid Glamorgan) 0656 768368.

Apex Paintball (Bangor) 0232 63778.

Valley Paintball Games (Aberdare) 0685 813422.

Fireball Combat (Newport) 0633 254316.

Mayhem Teamline (Swansea) 0639 730725.

Survival Game (UK) Limited 0269 822568.

SWAT Combat Games 0352 56916.

Task Force (South Wales) 0222 797064.

War Zone One (Swansea) 0792 645750.

Welsh Capital Combat Games (Cardiff) 0291 421403.

Dragon Valley Combat (Tyleri Valley) 0633 254316.

WARWICKSHIRE (ENGLAND)
Skirmish 0905 426313.
Skirmish (North Warwickshire) 0926 758682.
Survival Game (UK) Limited 0926 491948.

WASHINGTON (USA)
Evergreen Action Sports Inc, 15330 NE 114th H119, Bellevue, WA 98007 (206) 562 2670.
Northeast Paintball Adventure Land, So 1015 Bowdish, Spokane, WA 99206.
The Outback, Wa Box 697, Rainier, WA 98576 (206) 446 2345.
Peninsula Paintball, 249 Diamond Point Road, Sequim, WA 98382 (206) 683 1954.
Evergreen Action Supplies, 3901 NE 4th, Renton, WA 98056 (206) 228 9650.
Fun on the Run, 17022 South East 264, Kent, WA 98042 (206) 630 8965.
The Jolly Soldier, 902A NE 65th Street, Seattle, WA 98115 (208) 524 2266.
Max V 300, Black Diamond, WA (206) 467 0175.
Night Owl Gun Sales, 14915 Aurora Avenue, N Seattle, WA 98133 (206) 367 4997.
Northwest Adventure Games, 605 First Avenue, Suite 315, Seattle, WA 98104 (206) 467 0175.
Paint Pellet Park, Sultan, WA (206) 467 0175.
The Trak, Gig Harbor, WA (206) 467 0175.

WEST MIDLANDS (ENGLAND)
Capture The Flag 021 585 5270
Combat Leisure Game (UK) Limited (Birmingham) 021 770 7297.
Combat 2000 (Wolverhampton) 0902 313344.
DAI (Indoor Site) (West Midlands) 0384 265151.
Strike Force 0203 452869.
Mayhem Paintball Games Limited (Mayhem Encounters) 0203 461234.
Midland Paintball Centre 021 359 8927.
Kooh Doow (Fantasy Fields) 021 359 8927.
Kooh Doow (Tournament Fields) 0831 406479.
Skirmish (NE Birmingham) 021 758682.
Skirmish (S Birmingham) 021 426313.
Skirmish (NW Birmingham) 021 660646.
Splatoon 0384 76111.
Task Force 0928 33060.
The Combat Game (West Midlands) 021 430 4069.
The Adventure Game (Birmingham) 021 477 4326.
Trapshot (Express Ball) Brierley Hill 0384 265151.
War Zone (Stourbridge) 0384 456161.

WEST SUSSEX (ENGLAND)
California Commando (Brighton Site) 0273 484666.
Fireball Adventures (UK) Limited, Fireball Adventures (Sussex) 0323 843878.
Holmbush Outdoor Games Limited (Crawley) 0293 6623.
Skirmish 079 156644.
Splatt Sports 0903 830905.
Survival Game (UK) Limited (Hickstead) 0444 881479.
Target 0705 471107.
The Great Adventure Game 0903 892890.
Paintball Tactics Petworth Limited 0798 44128.

WEST YORKSHIRE (ENGLAND)
Paintball Adventures (Leeds) 0532 605438.
Paintball Commando 0924 252123.
Splatoon 0532 566550.
Top Gun 0274 734164.
Warpaint (Leeds) 0836 693662.

WILTSHIRE (ENGLAND)
Akal Paintball 0793 618877.
Mayhem Paintball Games Limited, Euro Wargames 0249 443088.
Paintball Adventure Game Supplies 0264 51570.
Skirmish 0985 40798.
Sports Encounters Leisure 0794 390590.
Survival Game (UK) Limited 0380 3559.

WISCONSIN (USA)
Paintball Dave's, 203 North Broadway, Milwaukee, WI 532002 (414) 271 3004.
Paintball Sam's, Highway K, Raymond, WI 53185.
The Ultimate Adventure Outfitters, PO Box 245, Oseola, WI 54020 (715) 755 3888.

Index